Renew by phone or online
0845 0020 777
www.bristol.gov.uk/libraries

KT-177-626

BRISTOL CITY COUNCIL
LIBRARY SERVICES
WITHDRAWN AND OFFERED FOR SALE
SOLD AS SEEN

Bristol Libraries
1800463777

containers

containers

simple projects
for the weekend gardener

George Carter

photography by Marianne Majerus

RYLAND
PETERS
& SMALL

LONDON NEW YORK

Designer *Sarah Walden*

Senior editor *Henrietta Heald*

Production *Patricia Harrington*

Art director *Gabriella Le Grazie*

Publishing director *Alison Starling*

Illustrations *Michael Hill*

First published in the United Kingdom in 1997
and reissued with amendments in 2004 by
Ryland Peters & Small
Kirkman House
12–14 Whitfield Street
London W1T 2RP
www.rylandpeters.com

10 9 8 7 6 5 4 3 2 1

Text copyright © George Carter 1997, 2004
Design, illustrations and photographs copyright
© Ryland Peters & Small 1997, 2004

The author's moral rights have been asserted.
All rights reserved. No part of this publication may
be reproduced, stored in a retrieval system, or
transmitted in any form or by any means, electronic,
mechanical, photocopying or otherwise, without the
prior permission of the publisher.

ISBN 1 84172 611 7

A CIP record for this book is available from
the British Library.

Printed and bound in China.

contents

introduction

Growing plants in containers, like all gardening, is a compromise between nature and artifice. It enables you to simulate all kinds of growing conditions, place plants wherever they are wanted, grow combinations that would be impossible together in the open ground, and overwinter tender plants under cover. Container growing also makes it possible to rearrange the outside look of your home in much the same way as you might rearrange the interior – whether radically to change the seasonal appearance or to transform a terrace for a new purpose.

The projects in this book are not confined to conventional containers. There are ideas for portable plant screens or hedges, for architectural containers, and for plant pots as gate piers. The designs not only show you how to grow in containers but also suggest how to place plants in an overall garden or backyard scheme.

There are innovative schemes for transforming ordinary window boxes, terracotta pots and wooden tubs: simple changes that make containers relate more closely to their setting and which elevate gardening to an activity that combines horticulture with exterior decoration.

George Carter

terracotta

There are many variations in the colour of terracotta – from the harsh red of new machine-made pots to the softer texture associated with hand-thrown pots. The 18th-century landscape gardener Humphry Repton used pale stone paints and limewashes to disguise red brick, which he thought too warm a colour against the various greens of the landscape. Paints can be used for various effects, including making a container appear more or less conspicuous. The combination of white, grey and blue shown opposite recalls the delft flower pots much used in 17th- and 18th-century gardens to set in rows on walls or terraces.

top A hand-thrown urn painted dark green has patinated to a mottled bronze. Planted with pinkish-blue hydrangeas, the urn looks best displayed above ground level on a painted wooden plinth.

above Clipped box (*Buxus sempervirens*) is a valuable container plant since its effect stays the same through the year. An underplanting of pink and purple petunias gives the box a colourful border in the summer flowering months. The petunias will need liquid-feeding to keep them going during the growing season in the face of competition from the box.

right The tall and distinctive shape of these pots is emphasized by their white-painted exteriors, which read better from a distance than darker terracotta.

above A wide urn-shaped pot suits the spreading habit of the variegated hosta (*Hosta sieboldiana* 'Frances Williams'), whose bold architectural foliage continues throughout the growing season, making it an asset even after the flowers have died off.

above right This large terracotta pot has been planted up for early spring with dark blue and white hyacinths.

right A painted stepladder makes a stage for a late spring/early summer display of felicia, drumstick primulas (*Primula denticulata*), marguerites (*Argyranthemum frutescens*) and double daises (*Bellis perennis*).

far right, above Machine-made terracotta pots have been painted in white, grey and blue emulsion. Choose plants that sit comfortably with the colour of your painted pot.

far right, below Dwarf tulips make a good spring plant for this simple terracotta pot. The double early *Tulipa* 'Schoonoord' shown here will provide long-lasting flowers in April.

patinated terracotta

Many modern terracotta pots, especially machine-made varieties, have a raw new
look that can detract from the effect of an attractive planting scheme. They can also look
out of place next to old containers that have softened with age. One answer is to tone
down new pots using special paint to simulate patinated terracotta. In this project
we show how to age a terracotta trough artificially by this method, and how to
display it effectively side by side with naturally patinated pots.

MATERIALS & EQUIPMENT

1 new terracotta trough 600 x 230 x 230 mm (24 x 9 x 9 in)

2 naturally patinated terracotta pots with 250 mm (10 in) diameter

small pot off-white or grey oil-bound distemper

small paintbrush

scrubbing brush

bucket

pot shards

20 litres loam-based compost

3 creeping soft grass (*Holcus mollis* 'Albovariegatus')

in 150 mm (6 in) diameter pots

2 box balls (*Buxus sempervirens*)

1   Prepare the paint by putting a tablespoon of distemper into 300 ml (½ pint) of cold water and mix well.

2   Coat the outside of the trough with this watered-down solution using the small-headed paintbrush. Make sure that you paint right into the curves and indents on the relief detail.

3   When the distemper is dry, scrub it off using a stiff brush dipped into a bucket of cold water. The object is to leave a white deposit in the relief detail and around the moulding edges, but to remove the paint from the flat surfaces almost entirely, except for the odd blemish. Don't worry about scrubbing off all the paint – what remains sinks into the pores of the terracotta, ensuring that a subtle colour variation remains.

   If necessary, apply another thin wash to the relief detail and scrub off again.

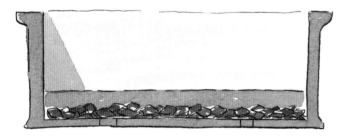

4   Fill the bottom of the trough to a depth of 20 mm (¾ in) with pot shards to help drainage. Cover this layer with enough loam-based compost to raise the top of the grass pots to 25 mm (1 in) below the top edge of the container.

5   Remove the grasses from their pots and place them on the compost layer, then fill the remaining space with compost, and firm down gently. Soak the compost and check often to make sure the soil has not dried out. After eight weeks or so apply a weak liquid fertilizer, and continue to feed on a monthly basis in spring, summer and autumn.

6   Plant up the two naturally patinated containers with the box balls, lining the base with pot shards and filling with compost, as for the trough.

7   Display these pots on either side of the trough. The naturally aged appearance of the terracotta pots develops only after several years of outdoor use, but the artificially patinated trough that has been instantly aged sits well between them.

alternative suggestion

For a more heavily patinated look, create an antiqued bronze appearance. This effect, although more complicated than the patinated effect, is still easy to achieve.

Create a glaze by mixing one part water to one part deep blue-green matt emulsion. Wipe it over the outside of the trough with a rag.

Create two more glazes as before with pale blue and pale green matt emulsion and apply them in random strokes using a small paint brush. Dip the brush in water and drag it around the rim, letting the water run down the trough in streaks. Allow to dry. Blend the glazes with fine-grade steel wool.

Finally, make a glaze with white matt emulsion and apply a thin coat to the surface of the trough; while the paint is still wet wipe it off with a damp cloth, leaving small deposits in the moulding and just enough to soften the blue and green colours.

painted pots

A good way of introducing vibrant colour to an ordinary terracotta pot is to paint it.
Paint also disguises the rather harsh-looking red appearance of so much machine-made
terracotta. Use the green and yellow scheme chosen here or pick your own combination to
match the architectural background of your garden. To create the greatest impact, paint
the pots in simple striking designs and pick plants to match the overall colour scheme.

MATERIALS & EQUIPMENT

machine-made terracotta pots: 2 with 230 mm (9 in) diameters,

2 with 170 mm (7 in) diameters, 2 with 150 mm (6 in) diameters

1 litre (1¾ pints) each yellow matt emulsion and palm-green matt emulsion

masking tape 25 mm (1 in) wide

paintbrush and watercolour brush

pot shards

30 litres general-purpose compost

10 lilies (*Lilium* 'Reinesse')

10 creamy *Osteospermum* 'Buttermilk'

6 lime-and-cream petunias

1   Begin by painting one of each size of pot in green; coat the outside and the top 40 mm (1½ in) on the inside. Repeat for the remaining pots using the yellow paint; you may find that it takes two coats of yellow to hide the terracotta colouring beneath. Wait for the paint to dry before applying the pattern.

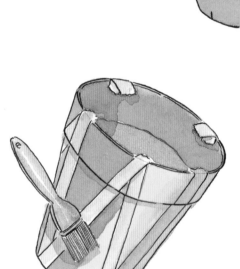

2   Use the largest pots for the zigzag design. Divide the circumference at the base into five equal parts and mark with a pencil. Then divide the top into five, placing these marks exactly midway between the ones already made around the base.

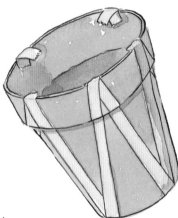

3   Apply the masking tape in strips, joining the top and bottom marks so that a zigzag pattern is formed on the outside of the pots.

4   On the outside, paint the green-based pot yellow, overlapping the edges of the masking tape, and paint the yellow-based pot green. Peel off the tape when the paint is completely dry to reveal a neat zigzag pattern.

5   Select another yellow pot and a green pot and decorate with 25 mm (1 in) diameter spots in the contrasting colour using a watercolour brush; draw freehand or make a template by cutting a circle out of a 100 mm (4 in) square of card and painting over it.
      Finish the pots by painting the top band in the same colour as the spots.

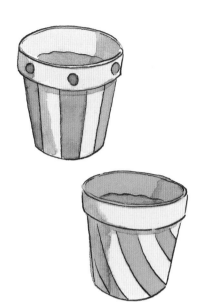

6 In this arrangement the other two pots have been left plain, but you can devise any pattern of your choice, remembering that simple bold designs work best. Here are some alternatives.

7 Use the larger pots for the lilies. 'Reinesse' is a stem-rooting lily so line the pot with pot shards and plant 150–200 mm (6–8 in) deep to allow for root development. If you choose a basal-rooting lily, such as *Lilium candidum*, plant 100–150 mm (4–6 in) deep. Plant bulbs from autumn to spring or pot-grown lilies any time. Fill in with compost, water and protect from frost.

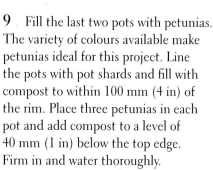

8 Line two more pots with pot shards and half fill with compost. Place five *Osteospermum* in each and fill with compost. Bring these plants indoors in the autumn and winter to protect them from frost.

9 Fill the last two pots with petunias. The variety of colours available make petunias ideal for this project. Line the pots with pot shards and fill with compost to within 100 mm (4 in) of the rim. Place three petunias in each pot and add compost to a level of 40 mm (1 in) below the top edge. Firm in and water thoroughly.

grouping terracotta pots

To achieve a satisfactory grouping of plants in pots requires planning. Stick to one material to give unity, but choose a variety of sizes and shapes. Mix textures and scales with seasonally changing flowers (see project for planting suggestions). Pick a plain background for a visually complex group, or a more decorative one for a simple bold display. The focus in this project is on the wide variety of pots and plants available for creating a group display. Follow the steps exactly or adapt the plants and pot sizes to suit the style and architecture of your garden.

MATERIALS & EQUIPMENT

large pot 350 mm (14 in) high with 400 mm (16 in) diameter

medium pot 250 mm (10 in) high with 250 mm (10 in) diameter

basket weave pot 350 mm (14 in) high with 350 mm (14 in) diameter

square container 350 mm (14 in)

small pot 170 mm (7 in) high with 250 mm (10 in) diameter

very large pot 400 mm (16 in) high with 450 mm (18 in) diameter

small cylinder with handles 300 mm (12 in) high with 350 mm (14 in) diameter

small shallow pan 130 mm (15 in) high with 300 mm (12 in) diameter

large shallow pan 170 mm (7 in) high with 450 mm (18 in) diameter

pot shards, manure and compost (see steps, opposite, for different types)

bamboo canes • garden ties • spiral-shaped wire frame (optional)

spring planting

1 Fill the large pot with a young *Polygala myrtifolia*, ideal for training. Line the container with pot shards and plant the root ball in soil-based compost. Support the leading stem on a cane and cut off the tip when it reaches about 550 mm (22 in) in height. Remove any lower shoots back to the stem and trim the ends of the horizontals to encourage bushiness. Once the required shape is achieved, clip annually to maintain uniformity. Bring inside over winter.

2 Plant the medium pot with hart's tongue fern (*Phyllitis scolopendrium*). Use a peat-based compost mixed with sand after lining the container with pot shards. Water regularly and bring inside over winter.

3 Plant a box (*Buxus sempervirens*) in the basket-weave pot; the simple shape of this plant sets off the patterned pot to its best advantage. Place a small pot-grown specimen in soil-based compost, over a layer of pot shards; keep well watered and feed with a slow release granular fertilizer and spray-on foliar feed, to encourage growth. As it grows pinch off the end shoots for a dense bushy effect and trim to create a ball shape.

4 In this arrangement two hostas have been chosen for their luscious foliage. Use the square container for a *Hosta sieboldiana* var. *elegans* and the small pot for a *Hosta fortunei* var. *aureomarginata*. Plant over pot shards in rich compost; use one part manure to three parts soil-based compost. Water regularly and apply liquid manure to plants in flower.

5 The evergreen small-leaved holly (*Ilex crenata*) is planted in the very large pot and makes an ideal subject for topiary. Choose a plant with a straight stem and plant in soil-based compost over a layer of pot shards. Tie the stem to a cane about 900 mm (36 in) long and grow into the shape of a pyramid. Once you have a dense pyramid of holly, trim to form a spiral.

Alternatively train the young stem onto a spiral wire frame, attaching it with garden ties. Pinch out the ends and trim to desired shape as before.

6 Next plant up the small cylinder with a *Hydrangea macrophylla* 'Blue Wave'. Line your pot with pot shards and plant in soil-based compost. Water well during the growing season and prune in autumn. The colour of this plant will vary according to soil type; more alkaline soils produce the pinker flowers, seen left.

summer planting

7 *Ageratum houstonianum* have been chosen for the small shallow pan. Buy five plants in 80 mm (3 in) pots; the colours range from blues and purples to pinks and whites. In late May line the pan with pot shards and arrange the de-potted plants in soil-based compost.

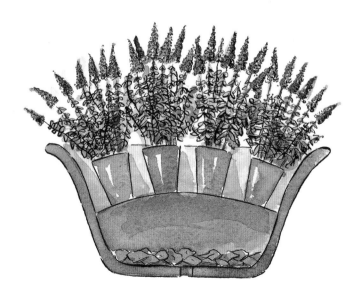

8 Finally, fill the large shallow pan with nine sage plants (*Salvia farinacea* 'Rhea'). Use a loam-based compost over pot shards. Space the plants so that the adult leaves will touch one another for a full display. Pinch out the tips of young shoots for a more bushy effect.

arranging the plants

See the photograph of the finished project on page 19. The taller plants create a backdrop of greenery for the colourful flowers in the foreground. For your own display you may wish to use steps or stages to create the right balance of height and bushiness.

masonry

Stone or marble containers, unless old, are difficult to find today, although they are still made in Italy to traditional designs. Cast concrete in various stone colours is more easily found. You can paint smooth surfaces in limewash or oil-bound distemper and allow more porous, pitted surfaces to patinate naturally.

top Oriental glazed ceramic pots offer good value and are usually elegantly shaped. They are also available in blue and white, which looks good outdoors. Space them out on a terrace as a repeat element.

above A cast-concrete trough looks best patinated or distressed to complement the asters. Encourage moss and mould by painting with liquid fertilizer and keep in a damp, shaded position.

right A concrete basket-weave pot of early 19th-century type echoes the basket-edged beds and actual basket planters often seen in Regency gardens. This sort of pot looks good raised on a low brick wall or wooden pier, displayed with pink geraniums.

far right This 1930s-style urn, on account of its simple outline, makes a useful centrepiece that will hold its own against a complex background. It is planted for summer with blue solenopsis.

top Lightweight fibreglass reinforced concrete containers are useful for roof terraces or where containers need to be moved around. This one has been planted with a smoke bush.

above A shallow glazed ceramic bonsai trough makes a useful container for a low planting of eustoma. Keep shallow containers well watered because they are more susceptible than deeper ones to drying out.

above right An unadorned glazed ceramic container makes an attractive foil for a *Lavatera trimestris* 'Pink Beauty', which is distinguished by its very pale pink flowers with purple veining and purple centres.

right This unusual pot has been cast to resemble an 18th-century water cistern and subsequently treated to look like lead. The pink of the hydrangeas sets up an interesting contrast.

vertical planting

Town gardens can often be improved by making them more private. One way to achieve this is to plant upwards. An ordinary hedge is a popular solution, but even on a roof terrace one can achieve more interesting screening effects using containers. This project shows how to get a banded effect of pleached lime underplanted with ivy, below which are containers for flowers. If you wish to enclose all the sides of your garden, simply add more troughs and trellis backing.

MATERIALS & EQUIPMENT

2 concrete troughs 600 x 450 x 450 mm (24 x 18 x 18 in)

1 concrete trough 450 x 450 x 450 mm (18 x 18 x 18 in)

dark green matt emulsion

section of trellis, 1.8 x 1.8 m (6 x 6 ft)

2 vertical wooden posts 2200 x 50 x 50 mm (84 x 2 x 2 in)

coated wire or garden ties and sea-washed pebbles

pot shards, soil-based compost and slow-release fertilizer

1 red-twigged lime (*Tilia platyphyllos* 'Rubra')

6 ivy plants (*Hedera helix*)

8 white petunias

8 purple *Verbena tenera*

8 white trailing *Verbena tenuisecta* f. *alba*

2 ferns (*Athyrium filix-femina*)

1   Start by securing the trellis backing. In this project vertical posts have been attached to the outside of a 300 mm (12 in) high parapet. If you don't have a wall, secure the posts in the ground. Space them 1.8 m (6 ft) apart so the trellis fits between them. Screw the trellis to the face of the posts 300 mm (12 in) above ground level. Or, if you have a high wall or wooden fence, you can train your plants along wires. Stretch plastic or galvanized wire horizontally between vine eyes at intervals and secure with screws.

2   Improve the appearance of the concrete troughs by coating in matt emulsion. Dark colours work best with this planting scheme.

3   Plant up the lime in the small square trough. Choose a pot-grown specimen with a dense root system and a straight stem, ideally about 1.8 m (6 ft) high with lateral branches at the top; plant in autumn or early spring.

4   Cover the drainage holes of your container with pot shards and line with compost. Ease the lime out of its pot and position it towards the back of the trough. Plant the ferns in front of the lime and work compost around the root balls, making sure that they are level, and fill in with compost to within 80 mm (3 in) of the top. Add a top dressing of slow-release fertilizer and decorate the surface with pebbles.

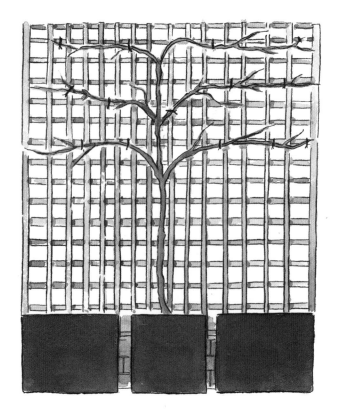

5   To achieve the striped effect at the top of the trellis, three lines of lateral branches have been trained horizontally. Start by choosing two strong laterals about 1.2 m (4 ft) from the base of the lime, on opposite sides of the stem. Secure them horizontally along the trellis with coated wire. Repeat for the next two lines, spacing them about 300 mm (12 in) apart.

6   Remove all the other side shoots from the stem and grow the trained laterals to the full width of the trellis. Prune annually and cut back excess foliage.

7　Next plant up the two larger troughs on each side of
the lime. Line the containers with pot shards and fill with
compost to within 80 mm (3 in) of the top. Choose a plain
green ivy with multiple stems that will provide a good
hedge-like effect. Position three ivies at the back of each
trough and top up with compost. If you want to create
a dense screen, you can train the ivy into a fan shape,
tying it to the trellis with coated wire.

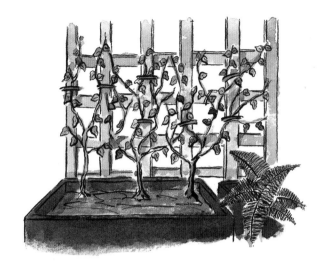

8　Grow the ivy to a height of 900 mm
(3 ft) and allow the plants in both troughs
to join together. Clip the ivy back to keep
it flat against the trellis and maintain a
straight line along the top; you don't want
the ivy to meet the lime since this would
make the banded effect less well defined.

9　Complete the large troughs with a
seasonal planting scheme. White petunias,
purple verbenas and white trailing verbenas
have been planted along the front to give a
long summer show. Keep well watered and
fed. To make a longer wall screen or enclose
a space, add to the number of troughs and
secure extra panels of trellis.

alternative planting schemes

Plant forget-me-nots (*Myosotis alpestris*) for a blue
haze in spring, or, for autumn, plant a pot-grown
cylamen such as C. *cilicium* or C. *hederifolium*.

planting schemes for urns

Urns are particularly popular in Italian gardens, where they form an integral
part of the garden architecture. They can be used effectively to punctuate a design
or standing alone to create a focal point; place them at intervals on walls and
balustrades, or display them high on gate piers and plinths.

MATERIALS & EQUIPMENT

shallow 'campagna'-shaped urn

pot shards

loam-based compost

plinth for display

10 houseleeks (*Sempervivum tectorum*)

bear's breeches (*Acanthus mollis*)

Cordyline indivisa

lemon tree (*Citrus limon* 'Meyer')

trailing *Lobelia*

1   The shallow shape of a 'campagna' urn complements the low-growing succulents used in this arrangement. Their shallow roots are not restricted by the container, making them an ideal choice.

Succulents need good drainage, so make sure that there are holes in the base of the urn to prevent waterlogging. Place a layer of pot shards in the bottom of the container to improve drainage further.

2   Fill the urn with a loam-based potting compost until it forms a dome-shaped mound above the rim. Thoroughly soak the compost.

3   Begin by planting the small houseleeks, positioning them at intervals of about 80 mm (3 in). It is advisable to keep the plants well watered, although succulents can survive drought conditions and will continue to grow even on a gate pier that is too high for watering.

4   As plants develop from the individual houseleeks, the surface will become covered, forming an unbroken mass. To enhance the display, allow the plants to spill over the edge on their aerial roots.

5   The sculpted effect produced by the sharp green leaves and tight rosettes looks best on a plinth; choose one of the same material as the urn or one of painted wood.

alternative planting schemes

right A tall urn matches the proportions of the *Acanthus mollis* with its spikes of funnel-shaped flowers surrounded by deeply cut leaves.

above This Art Deco urn has been planted with trailing *Lobelia*. The profusion of pale blue flowers contrasts with the urn's clearly defined ridges.

left The size and shape of the Baroque urn suit a small lemon tree (*Citrus limon* 'Meyer'); the narrow neck helps the tree to retain the moisture it needs.

above A large neoclassical urn has been chosen for the *Cordyline indivisa*, which needs room to spread.

a brickwork trough

A tall brick structure creates a stronger visual impact than could be achieved by an urn or
a small planter. This trough provides the opportunity for a stunning display of flowering and
non-flowering plants, which should nevertheless be simple enough to appreciate from a distance.
The trough can be used for a mixture of permanent structural planting and seasonal bedding
out – and will act as an important focal point in the garden all year round.

MATERIALS & EQUIPMENT

foundations: a small bag of cement, 50 kg (1 cwt) aggregate, 25 kg (½ cwt) sharp sand

mortar: a small bag of cement, 50 kg (1 cwt) soft sand

105 frost-resistant bricks (Old Cheshires have been used here)

1 piece 450 x 450 x 10 mm (18 x 18 x ½ in) exterior-grade plywood

4 concrete blocks 450 x 230 x 100 mm (18 x 9 x 4 in)

30 litres no. 2 potting compost

1 half-standard rose (*Rosa* 'Sanders' White Rambler')

4 *Hebe pinguifolia* 'Pagei'

18 tobacco plants (*Nicotiana alata* 'Lime Green')

barrow • bricklayer's trowel • pegs • spirit level • string

1   The trough needs to be built on foundations 130 mm (5 in) deep. Excavate a 825 mm (33 in) square hole to this depth. If your trough is to be sited on a gravel path, rake away the gravel from the area before digging your hole.

2   About two barrowloads of concrete are needed for the foundations. The ratio of the mix is six aggregate to three sharp sand and one cement. Mix these dry ingredients on a plywood board. Make a well in the centre and start to add water. Mix to form a stiff cohesive paste and transfer the concrete to a barrow.

3   Tip the concrete into the prepared hole, spreading it right into the corners. Level off with a straight-edged board and make sure there are no air pockets; use a spirit level to check that the surface is horizontal. Leave to dry out for at least 24 hours, and preferably several days, using a polythene sheet to protect it from the weather.

4   Mark out 680 mm (27 in) square with string and pegs, 65 mm (2½ in) above the concrete bed, to guide the first course of bricks.

5   Make the mortar as for the concrete (see step 2) using the ratio of four parts soft sand to one part cement. Spread a 10 mm (½ in) thick layer on the slab.

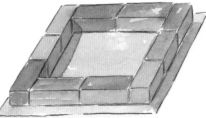

6   Position the bricks according to the plan. Lay the first course with the 'frog' at the top, butting all brick ends with mortar. Place the second layer staggered over the joints on the first. After this and later courses, remove excess mortar from the joints, flush with the brick face, and point.

7   Continue to build the container until it has nine layers of brick; make sure that the face and height are even by checking at regular intervals with a spirit level.

8   Complete the trough with a coping course, stepping out the brick by 25 mm (1 in) to create a top moulding. Four filler pieces 100 x 50 mm (4 x 2 in) are needed to stretch the coping over the edges.

9   Fill the inside corners of the step with concrete to strengthen the join.

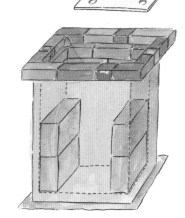

10   To avoid having to fill the entire container with compost, make a plywood stage. First drill five 25 mm (1 in) diameter holes in the wood for drainage. Then place the four concrete blocks inside the structure and rest the plywood over them.

11   For the following planting plan, the hebes and half-standard rose remain in their plastic pots but are set in soil, whereas the tobacco plants are de-potted and planted directly into the compost.

12   Position the rose in the centre, below the level of the top of the container, then fill with enough compost to sit the hebes flush with the coping layer. Finally, fill in the spaces with compost, placing the tobacco plants around the rose. Keep the display well watered and use a liquid feed weekly.

alternative planting schemes

For winter, plant a half-standard holly (*Ilex* x *meserveae* 'Blue Prince') with ivy (*Hedera helix* 'Erecta'); for autumn, a *Pittosperum tenuifolium* 'Purpureum' with cyclamen (*C. cilicium*); and for spring a box cone (*Buxus sempervirens*) with a hyacinth (*Hyacinthus orientalis* 'Delft Blue') border.

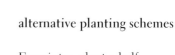

a circular pipe with flowering tree

In a paved garden or where soil is not available, large shrubs or small trees can be
grown in broad concrete pipes – an inexpensive solution for containing soil and
displaying plants. Here a decorative niche gives height to the arrangement and frames
the cascading flowers of the fuchsia plant with its frothy mass of underplanting.

MATERIALS & EQUIPMENT

1 section of concrete drainage pipe 500 mm (20 in) high

with a 900 mm (36 in) diameter

dark blue-green matt emulsion

pot shards

50 litres no. 3 potting compost

slow-release fertilizer

standard weeping *Fuchsia* x *speciosa* 'La Bianca'

10 lady's mantle (*Alchemilla mollis*)

6 pelargoniums (*P.* 'Friesdorf')

1   Choose a concrete drainage pipe to fit the size of the plant. The dimensions given on page 60 are suitable for a small to medium shrub. Conceal the rough surface of the pipe with a fresh coat of paint; dark blue-green harmonizes well with most garden schemes.

2   Position the painted pipe in your garden – it will rest equally comfortably on either a hard or a soft surface. Fill the base of the pipe to a depth of 30–50 mm (1–2 in) with pot shards; this will help to improve drainage.

3   If your weeping fuchsia is in a pot, carefully remove it and tease out any enmeshed roots. Fill the base of the pipe with enough compost to cover the pot shards. When you have finished planting, all the plants should be at the depth they were in the pots (see illustration). Add fertilizer as you plant.

4   Add compost to bring the plants and surrounding soil to a level about 40 mm (1½ in) below the rim of the pipe.

5   Place the fuchsia in the centre of the pipe. Again, the surface of the soil should be about 40 mm (1½ in) from the top of the pipe.

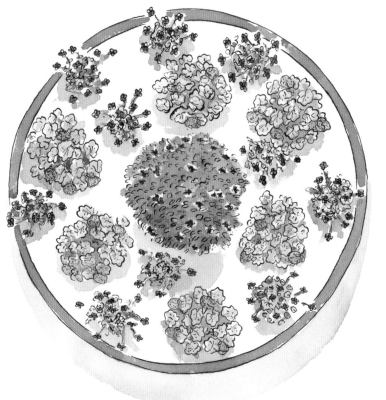

6 Underplant with lady's mantle and pelargoniums, placing them around the edge of the container in the positions shown in the illustration.

7 Pack the soil firmly around all the plants and water thoroughly. Monitor the container for water, especially during hot weather.

alternative planting scheme

Use two pipes of different diameters to achieve a stepped effect, inspired by medieval garden designs. Plant your tree in the central pipe and fill in the lower level with a seasonal planting scheme. This alternative planting display uses a weeping mulberry (*Morus alba* 'Pendula') above a bed of chamomile (*Anthemis nobile* 'Treneague').

a shell-faced trough

A simple decorative treatment refines the look of a concrete garden trough. Aluminium leaf adds a shiny surface to the shells but any metal leaf works well – the most extravagant-looking option being gold. Blue tones have been chosen for the planting arrangement since they complement the silvery-grey of the trough and shells. If you pick your own display, try to stick to one colour – a mixture may detract from the decorative impact of the container.

MATERIALS & EQUIPMENT

plain concrete trough 600 x 250 mm (24 x 10 in)

5 large scallop shells

1 litre (1¾ pints) dark grey undercoat

small jar Japan goldsize and aluminium leaf

paintbrush

two-part resin and hardener adhesive

30 litres potting compost

pot shards

pot-grown plants in 80–100 mm (3–4 in) pots, as follows:

5 *Delphinium belladonna* 'Wendy'

3 Cherry-pie heliotrope (*H. peruvianum* 'Royal Marine')

5 *Laurentia axillaris* 'Blue Star'

5 *Aptenia cordifolia* 'Variegata'

1   Paint the four sides of the trough and the first 25 mm (1 in) inside the top edge with the undercoat.

2   Pick five large scallops of roughly the same size; these can be purchased at a fishmonger's or a decorating shop. Clean and dry them thoroughly before applying the treatment. Paint the convex side with a single coat of undercoat.

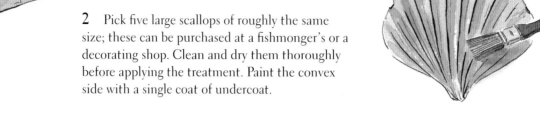

3   When the undercoat on the shells has dried, paint over it with the goldsize. Wait until the surface is almost dry but still slightly tacky before attaching the metal leaf.

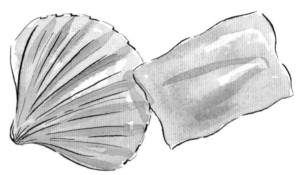

4   Apply the transfer leaf over the tacky surface of the shell; test that the adhesive is ready by placing a corner of the transfer onto the shell; if it instantly adheres, the shell is ready to take the leaf.

5   Attach the foil to the rest of the shell, rub it down lightly with cotton wool and peel back the transfer tissue. To achieve a distressed appearance, adhere the leaf to the raised areas of the shell; to do this, stretch the transfer over the upper surface and rub the top ridges only so that when you remove the backing the leaf has not stuck in the indents. Repeat for all five shells.

6   Mark the positions for the shells on the front and sides of the trough with a coloured pencil or a strip of masking tape; make your mark where the centre of the shell will sit. Site one shell centrally on each side of the trough and three spaced equidistantly on the front panel.

7   Now the trough and shells are ready to be joined. Mix the two-part adhesive – you will need an amount roughly the size of a golf ball. Using the applicator or a small wooden spatula, apply generous blobs of the glue to the inside edges of the shells in four or five places, as shown.

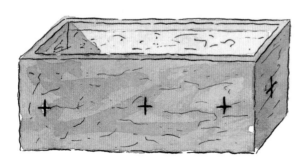

8 Tip the trough onto its side so that the front face is pointing upwards. Press each shell onto the three marked positions along the top and remove any glue spilling out from the sides with a clean applicator.

9 When the glue has dried, turn the trough back onto its base and fix the side shells; hold these in position while the adhesive sets.

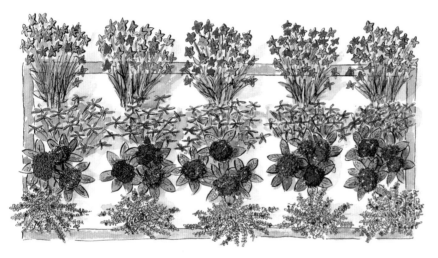

10 Put the trough in a sunny place and plant it up in June, using the scheme on the left as a guide. The plants have been positioned in rows and staggered to fit. The delphiniums are positioned at the back, followed by the laurentias; the heliotropes and the aptenias along the front.

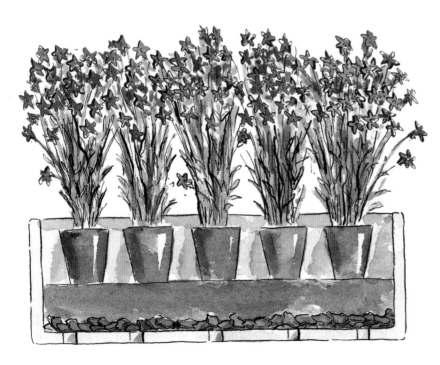

11 Cover the drainage holes with pot shards and fill the trough about half full with potting compost. Place the back row of delphiniums first and work your way forwards. Fill in with potting compost to within 25 mm (1 in) of the top edge, then firm in and water.

alternative planting schemes

For spring, plant *Convolvulus sabatius* with *Vinca minor* 'Alba Variegata'; in winter, fill the trough with winter-flowering pansies.

metal

Lead is one of the most beautiful metals and has the advantage that it patinates naturally outdoors; fixing sheet lead to a timber framework is much cheaper than using solid cast lead. Cast iron can look attractive if left to rust, but it is usually painted – dark colours tend to be more effective than light ones; before applying any paint to cast iron, it is important to prime the surface against corrosion. Galvanized steel or wirework is another finish that can be used to create decorative effects in outdoor plantings; it can either be painted or left in its original greyish-silver reflective state. If you want to add a touch of glitter to a metal container, apply a gold-leaf or silver-leaf detail.

right A 19th-century-style wirework stand proves useful for displaying a seasonally changing mix of plants in terracotta pots. Ferns combine well with white annuals. Paint wirework a colour that will show up against its background – here a dark colour has been used to read against a pale blue wall.

below A tall galvanized pot is shown off to best advantage by seasonal planting in a raised plastic liner. Lilies have been chosen for a late spring to early summer planting – their architectural lines complement the slender, upright shape of this particular container.

above This shallow wirework basket is overflowing with coleus – the tender foliage plant that was loved by the Victorians for its rich, rather artificial-looking variegated colours, reminiscent of the damasks of the period.

above right A deep galvanized potato picker painted in a dark green gloss makes an attractive jardinière for larger seasonally changed plants. Here it has been planted up with yellow *Lilium* 'Reinesse' – leave the lilies in their plastic pots so that they can easily be changed at the end of the flowering season.

right These osteospermums in a shallow galvanized tub will have a long summer flowering season. They are now available in a wide colour range and with different petal shapes.

top A tall 'campagna'-shaped urn can take a taller mass of planting than the shallower type of urn. From summer through to early autumn, dahlias provide a colourful display reminiscent of the late 19th century.

above Herbs can frequently be grown to eye-catching decorative effect in containers. In this case, a prostrate rosemary has been planted in an ornate metal goblet. The herb's curving branches and tiny pale blue flowers are in perfect harmony with the swirls on the cup.

a wirework basket

This unusual wirework basket is more of an enclosure than a container; such edgings were
used in the early 19th century to surround and support plants. A galvanized-iron strip
at the bottom creates a border around a basket-like stand that acts as an attractive frame for
rambling rose bushes. The best roses to use for this project are low-growing ground-cover
ones, but you can adapt the basket to fit larger plants such as shrub roses.

MATERIALS & EQUIPMENT

1 sheet galvanized steel 1200 x 300 mm (48 x 12 in); use a gauge that can be cut with tinsnips

6 galvanized roofing bolts, 10 mm ($1/2$ in) long and 6 mm ($1/4$ in) wide

22 m (72 ft) of galvanized fencing wire 5 mm ($1/5$ in) thick

1 piece plywood 525 x 350 x 25 mm (21 x 14 x 1 in)

tinsnips

hacksaw and vice or G-cramps

small pot grey-blue metal primer

roll of thin galvanized wire

well-rotted manure and rose fertilizer

5 bare-root roses (*Rosa* 'The Fairy')

1 Cut the sheet of galvanized iron into three strips, each 100 mm (4 in) wide. Cut two strips to a length of 1200 mm (48 in) and one to a length of 600 mm (24 in).

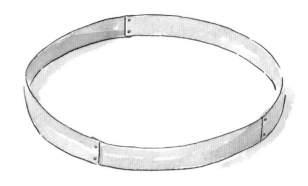

2 Drill two holes 7 mm (³/s in) in diameter at the ends of each strip. Then connect the three sections together to form a ring by lining up the holes at the ends and securing the joins with roofing bolts through the prepared holes. This strip acts as a template for preparing the bed and as a retainer for the basket.

3 For the basket, cut the fencing wire into sixteen pieces, each 1360 mm (54 in) long; use a hacksaw and vice or G-cramp to hold the wire in place.

4 To shape the wire, make a former from the plywood – this will act as a solid pattern around which to bend your wire. Mark the centre point at the top and draw the curved sides to within 200 mm (8 in) of the bottom; this section of the arch remains straight. Cut out the shape with a jigsaw.

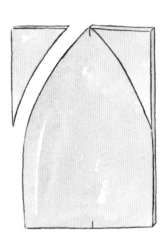

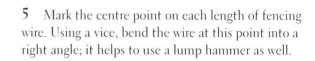

5 Mark the centre point on each length of fencing wire. Using a vice, bend the wire at this point into a right angle; it helps to use a lump hammer as well.

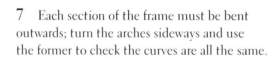

6 Place the right angle of wire over the tip of the former and bend the wire to fit the shape exactly; the wire should extend for about 100 mm (4 in) beyond the bottom edge of the former.

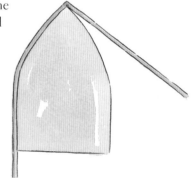

7 Each section of the frame must be bent outwards; turn the arches sideways and use the former to check the curves are all the same.

8 Before constructing the basket shape, paint all the metal components with the metal primer; grey-blue used here appears as a patinated copper colour and makes a good foil for this particular planting scheme.

9 Choose an area of flat ground for your rose bed. If the area is grassed over, position the ring and cut around its inner edge to mark the turf; put the ring to one side and remove the turf by dividing it into squares and lifting out with a spade. Turn over the bed and fork in well-rotted manure, then gently press the ring in position.

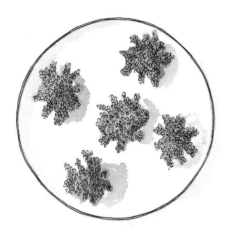

10 Plant the five roses, positioning them according to the planting plan on the left. Make sure that the junctions of stem and root are at surface level. Top dress with rose fertilizer.

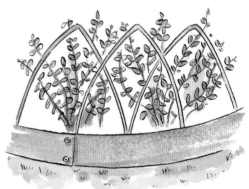

11 Insert the first arch hard up against the inner edge of the ring with the tip bending outwards and push it about 150–200 mm (6–8 in) into the ground. Insert the next arch so that it overlaps the original one by half its width. Repeat this process for the remaining arches all the way round the circumference; you may need to readjust the spacing on some of the arches for a neat and even fit.

12 Secure the basket sections together by twisting the thin galvanized wire around the crossover junctions on each arch.

13 Prune the roses so that they form a slightly domed shape and trim any grass around the outer edge for a formal effect.

alternative planting schemes

For a basket of this size, try the roses 'White Pet' or 'Nozomi', or for a larger arrangement use the pink rose 'Marguerite Hilling' or its creamy white sister 'Nevada'. A suitable shrub would be *Camellia japonica* 'Alba Plena'.

galvanized buckets

Hanging galvanized buckets on 'S' hooks is an inexpensive and attractive way of
displaying plants. A bright and vibrant arrangement, such as the one used here, adds a
splash of colour, decoration and movement to a blank expanse of wall in a simple setting.
Pick similar flowers in sharp colours and bold shapes to contrast with the plain outline and shiny
silver-grey surface of the buckets. For quick results, buy container-grown plants.

MATERIALS & EQUIPMENT

3 galvanized buckets 300 mm (12 in) in diameter

3 substantial galvanized angle brackets with tops 220 mm (8½ in) long and

sides 250 mm (10 in) long

3 threaded eye bolts with nuts to fit the holes in the angle brackets

3 'S' hooks, 80 mm (3 in)

no. 10 plated screws 50 mm (2 in)

pot shards

15 litres loam-based compost

4 African marigolds (*Tagetes erecta*)

2 pot marigolds (*Calendula officinalis*)

2 *Artemisia* 'Powys Castle'

2 single chrysanthemums

2 cone flowers (*Rudbeckia hirta*)

1 To prepare the buckets for planting, drill three drainage holes in the base of each one.

2 Line the bottom of each bucket with a layer of pot shards 25 mm (1 in) thick.

3 Fill the buckets about two-thirds of the way up with a loam-based free-draining compost. Then place four de-potted plants in each, making sure that the root ball is 25 mm (1 in) below the top edge of the bucket. Fill in with soil around the edges, lightly covering the surface of the root balls, and firm in. Give the plants a good soaking.

4 Choose a suitable location for your buckets. The plants used in this project need plenty of sun, so make sure your display area is in a sunny spot – a south-facing wall is ideal. Mark the position of each bracket on the wall with a pencil. In the example shown, the brackets have been staggered up a wall to allow space for plants to spread.

To fix the brackets to a stone wall, follow step 5. To fix the brackets to timber clapboard, follow step 6.

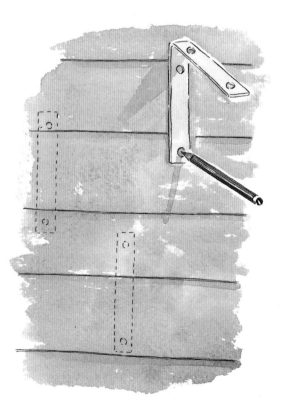

5 Screws and appropriate rawlplugs should be used for a masonry wall. Drill the holes for them with an electric drill and masonry bit.

6 For timber, use posidriv screws. If possible, fix the screws into a vertical studwork member behind the clapboard.

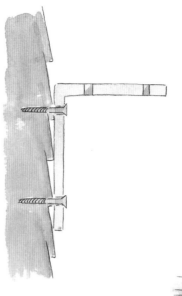

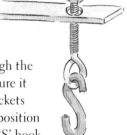

7 Put the threaded bolt through the end hole on the bracket and secure it with a nut; the height of the buckets can be altered by adjusting the position of the nut. Insert the end of an 'S' hook into the eye of the bolt.

8 This bucket has been planted with rudbeckias and chrysanthemums. It is especially important to keep all the plants well watered because the containers dry out quickly. Check daily if possible.

alternatives

Bring a burst of sunshine to a bare wall by filling your buckets with dwarf sunflowers (*Helianthus*), *Coreopsis tinctoria* and *Gazania* 'Orange Beauty'.

a lead-faced trough

Lead patinates to a beautiful silvery-grey colour – an effect that is simple and quick to achieve. You can simulate the appearance of a lead container by fixing sheet lead to a timber framework. Take care over size and placement; a window box must sit within the frame and be secured on brackets. Before embarking on this project, ensure that this style of container is in sympathy with the character and architecture of your building.

MATERIALS & EQUIPMENT

wooden box 950 x 250 x 230 mm (38 x 10 x 9 in), treated inside
and out with wood preservative

2 pieces softwood 285 x 30 x 30 mm (11^{1}/$_{4}$ x 1^{1}/$_{4}$ x 1^{1}/$_{4}$ in)

1 piece softwood 1030 x 30 x 30 mm (40^{1}/$_{2}$ x 1^{1}/$_{4}$ x 1^{1}/$_{4}$ in)

no. 8 screws 40 mm (1^{1}/$_{2}$ in)

galvanized clout nails 20 mm (^{3}/$_{4}$ in)

1 bottle white malt vinegar

gauge 4 lead 1430 x 250 mm (57 x 10 in) and 1550 x 130 mm (62 x 5 in)

6 *Senecio cineraria*

5 *Petunia* 'Ruby'

4 *Osteospermum* 'Whirly Gig'

3 pink bellflower (*Campanula carpatica*)

3 *Nemesia caerulea*

3 Persian violet (*Exacum affine*)

1 Put on protective gloves before handling the lead, and wash your hands afterwards. Cut with tinsnips.

2 Attach the wider strip of lead to one side of the box, top and bottom, with the galvanized clout nails.

3 Wrap the lead round to the front and planish the corner with a mallet to achieve a sharp corner.

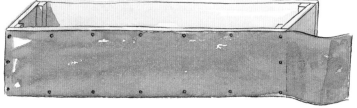

4 Nail the front in place, top and bottom, at 100–150 mm (5–6 in) intervals. Planish the other corner and nail the remaining side in place.

5 Take the three sections of softwood and mitre one corner on the short pieces and both corners on the longer one. Fit the sections together to form the moulding around the front and sides of the box, flush with the top edge. Drill holes for the screws around this edge and screw the moulding in place from the inside.

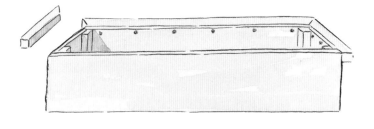

6 Take the second strip of lead and score a line along its length, using a nail and straight edge, 60 mm (2¼ in) down from the top. Divide the bottom into 31 sections of 50 mm (2 in), then divide the scored line into sections of the same size but starting 25 mm (1 in) in from the short end.

7   Join the marks up to form a zigzag pattern and then cut it out using tinsnips.

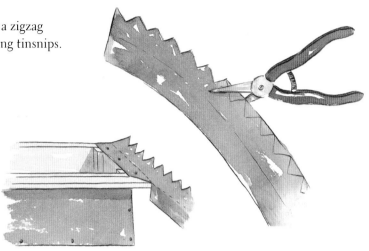

8   Place the straight edge of the cut-out along the inner edge of the box on the side. Nail it in place. In order to planish the strip neatly around the corner cut out a 90° notch from the lead, making sure that the corner point lines up exactly with the corner of the moulding. Hammer down the zigzag edge on the side and wrap the lead to the front of the box.

9   Now planish the top of the front section so that the zigzag sits neatly along the outside of the moulding. Nail in place. Complete the lead-facing for the last side, following the method already used.

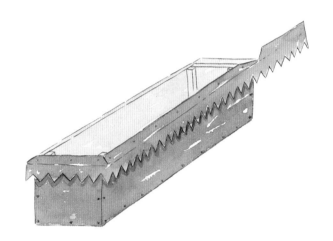

10   To give the box a patinated look apply white malt vinegar to the surface of the lead using a damp cloth. Keep applying until a mottled whitish-grey effect appears.

11   If your window sill slopes, make wedges to level the base of the box. Fix the box in place by screwing the inside of the box to the window frame or fixing retaining brackets to the front of the sill.

12   Line the box with pot shards and half fill with compost. Identify the plant positions by matching colours and numbers listed on page 54. Fill in with compost to 25 mm (1 in) below the top, firm in and water.

a wirework hanging basket

A 19th-century wirework basket makes an attractive hanging display. This one is particularly large, making it all the more striking. Anything larger would be impractical on account of the weight of the plants and soil. Site it on its own between an upstairs window and a door, or place one either side of a front door as a welcoming display.

MATERIALS & EQUIPMENT

wirework basket 600 mm (24 in) in diameter

no. 10 posidriv plated screws 40 mm (1½ in) and rawlplugs

galvanized angle bracket with top 350 mm (14 in) long

threaded eye bolt with nuts to fit angle bracket and large 'S' hook

peat- or fibre-based lightweight compost and sphagnum moss

pot-grown plants in 80 mm (3 in) plastic pots as follows:

10 *Petunia surfina*

5 *Fuchsia* 'Margaret'

5 pelargoniums (*P.* 'Balcon Royale')

6 *Petunia* 'Express Ruby'

6 heliotropes (*Heliotropium peruvianum*)

6 tobacco plants (*Nicotiana* 'Domino Pink')

1   You can buy decorative cast-iron shelf brackets, but for an elaborate basket such as this one it is better to use a plain bracket painted to match the wall surface.

Attach the bracket to the wall using screws and rawlplugs. When choosing a position, consider ease of hanging and watering, and when fixing make sure the bracket is firmly in place, particularly when hanging a basket over a path or in a doorway.

2   Push the threaded bolt through the end hole in the bracket and secure it with a nut, then insert the 'S' hook into the edge of the bolt for hanging the basket chain.

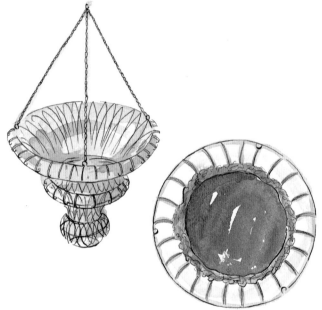

3   It is easier to work on the basket if you place it in a bucket – or hang it on a rope from a garage or shed door lintel or between a pair of folding steps.

Pushing the moss into the bottom of the container to a depth of 25 mm (1 in) and place a layer of compost over it to keep it in place. Continue lining the basket with moss, filling it with compost as you go, until the frame has been covered up to the top edge.

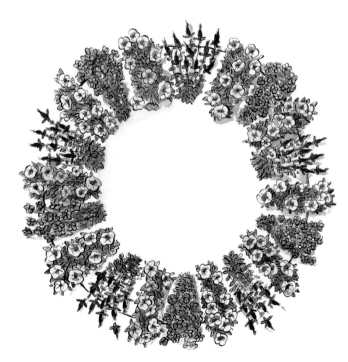

4   The plants used here are for a summer display; plant in late May. Start with the trailing specimens around the edge: the 10 petunias, the fuchsias and the pelargoniums. Position them according to the plan; lean them slightly outwards to follow the angle of the basket; keep them close together but with a thin layer of compost between each and around the outside edge.

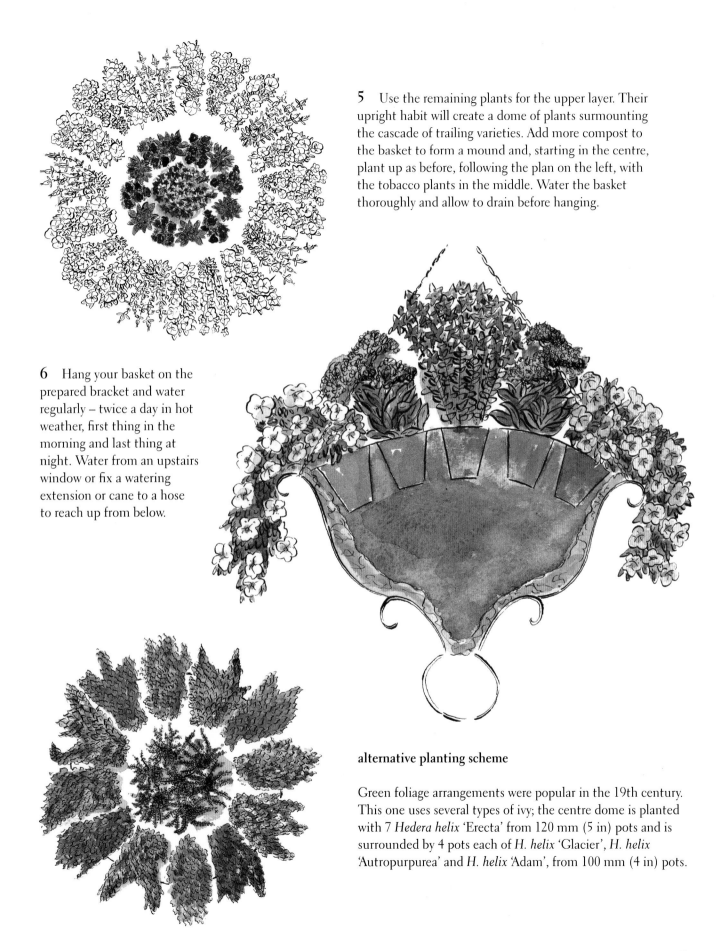

5 Use the remaining plants for the upper layer. Their upright habit will create a dome of plants surmounting the cascade of trailing varieties. Add more compost to the basket to form a mound and, starting in the centre, plant up as before, following the plan on the left, with the tobacco plants in the middle. Water the basket thoroughly and allow to drain before hanging.

6 Hang your basket on the prepared bracket and water regularly – twice a day in hot weather, first thing in the morning and last thing at night. Water from an upstairs window or fix a watering extension or cane to a hose to reach up from below.

alternative planting scheme

Green foliage arrangements were popular in the 19th century. This one uses several types of ivy; the centre dome is planted with 7 *Hedera helix* 'Erecta' from 120 mm (5 in) pots and is surrounded by 4 pots each of *H. helix* 'Glacier', *H. helix* 'Autropurpurea' and *H. helix* 'Adam', from 100 mm (4 in) pots.

61

a painted galvanized washtub

A galvanized tin or enamel bath can be turned into an elegant planter by adding ball feet
to give it the look of an early 19th-century jardinière. This planter is good for a large mass of
seasonal bedding and looks effective either on the ground or raised on a low plinth or wall.
Paint up to suit the colour of your plants and surroundings.

MATERIALS & EQUIPMENT

oval tin bath 600 mm (24 in) long and 450 mm (18 in) wide

1 piece exterior-grade plywood 450 x 350 x 18 mm (18 x 14 x ¾ in)

4 turned wooden balls with 65 mm (2½ in) diameter and

4 separate 7 mm (⅜ in) diameter dowels 50 mm (2 in) long

glue (waterproof PVA)

small jar Japan goldsize

1 packet or twelve 50 x 50 mm (2 x 2 in) squares gold leaf or Dutch metal

½ litre (1 pint) each clear wood preservative and dark red undercoat

1 litre (1¾ pints) matt emulsion

30 litres no. 2 potting compost and a bag of moss

36 dwarf pink and red tobacco plants (*Nicotiana* Domino Series)

1   Begin by making a plywood base in the recessed stand underneath the tub; this forms a fixing for the feet. Mark the shape of the base onto the plywood.

2   Draw a second oval about 5 mm (1/4 in) inside the first. Cut out the inner shape using a jigsaw.

3   Drill a 7 mm (3/8 in) diameter hole about halfway through each of the wooden balls, making sure it is straight and central.

4   Dribble a little glue inside these holes and insert the dowels so that they stick out about 25 mm (1 in) above the surface of the balls.

5   Paint the feet with clear wood preservative. When it has dried, apply two coats of dark red undercoat to simulate the colour of red gesso, which will give the finished effect a warm glow. Sand between each coat.

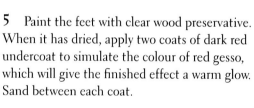

6   When the undercoat has completely dried, brush on a layer of goldsize. The goldsize needs to be almost dry to the touch before you apply the gold leaf.

7   Place the gold leaf over the tacky surface of the balls. Smooth over the backing surface before carefully peeling it off, leaving a layer of gold. Continue to apply the gold leaf, overlapping subsequent sheets, until the entire surface of each ball is covered. Rub off excess gold leaf but don't worry if the surface is uneven – this adds to the antique effect.

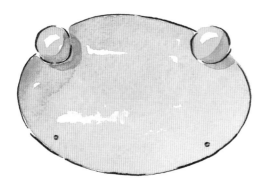

8   Drill four 7 mm (⅜ in) diameter holes into the plywood base to fit the dowels, positioning two at each end of the oval shape, close to the edge.Glue the dowels into the holes, pushing them in until the ball is touching the plywood base.

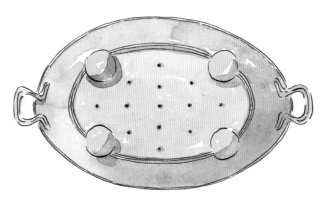

9   Insert the wooden base into the recessed stand of the washtub. Then drill a few small holes through the base of the tub and the plywood stand to ensure good drainage.

10   If your tub is a suitable colour, you may wish to leave it. However, both enamel and tin can be painted to suit a particular planting scheme. Gilding looks best against dark colours; navy-blue matt emulsion has been used here.

11   Fill the tub with compost to 130 mm (5 in) below the top, forming a slightly dome-shaped surface. Remove the tobacco plants from their pots and arrange them in the tub; for a colourful and dense mound of flowers, mix up the reds and pinks and position the root balls close together. Fill in the gaps with the remaining compost, firm in and keep well watered. Place the moss around the plants to help to retain moisture and for neatness.

alternative planting scheme

Place the tub indoors, in a kitchen or conservatory, or raise it on a plinth and plant with trailing ivy (*Hedera helix*).

wood

Wood provides the most varied selection of
containers, from a formal 17th-century Versailles
case to metal-banded coopered tubs. A wooden
surface should be painted or stained – unless it is
oak, which will weather to a pleasant silver-grey.

left This twig-work container planted with soleirolia is a variant on 19th-century rustic work. The sculpted character of this planter means that simple shapes and colours work best, allowing the design to be fully appreciated.

below left and far left A box standard and a chrysanthemum trained as a standard (far left) both make well-defined formal plantings for a Versailles case. Place cases in pairs flanking a front door or the entrance to a formal terrace or garden.

below The clump-forming perennial *Sedum spectabile*, shown here in a shallow wooden box, is a very useful container plant; its mass of foliage is as attractive as its compact, yellow-centred flower heads.

opposite, above left Evergreen shrubs create a dark green mound in this tall coopered tub. Purpose-made coopered tubs tend to be better proportioned than half-barrels. If the steel bands are not galvanized, paint them to reduce rusting.

opposite, above centre A panelled wooden window box has been planted with variegated ivy and *Capsicum annuum* 'Holiday Time'. Place at ground level on a paved terrace to act as a narrow border.

opposite, above right A Victorian shoe-cleaning box has found a new life as an eye-catching planter filled with chrysanthemums. If a box of this kind has not been painted or finished, treat it with wood preservative before planting up.

opposite, below A shallow coopered tub has been planted with the poached egg plant (*Limnanthes douglasii*), which provides a useful mass of low white-yellow flowers to complement the water plants.

a rustic Regency window box

The fashion for producing objects covered in barked wood started in the 18th century. This design is based on the style of the Regency landscape gardener Humphry Repton, who imitated the forms of classical architecture using rustic materials such as barked columns and pine-cone festoons.

MATERIALS & EQUIPMENT

exterior-grade plywood and planed softwood (see step 1, page 70)

1 litre (1³/4 pints) each clear wood preservative and green wood stain

4.3 m (14 ft) halved barked poles with 50–65 mm (2–2¹/2 in) diameter

3 large and 8 small pine cones

no. 8 screws 20 mm (1¹/2 in)

galvanized clout nails 80 mm (3 in)

sheradized panel pins 50 and 65 mm (2 and 2¹/2 in)

pot shards

30 litres peat-based compost

3 male ferns (*Dryopteris filix-mas*)

6 crested female ferns (*Athyrium filix-femina cristatum*)

9 white cup flowers (*Nierembergia*)

small bag of sphagnum moss

1   Cut the following in exterior-grade plywood:
• 2 pieces for front and back 900 x 250 x 18 mm
   (36 x 10 x ¾ in)
• 2 pieces for sides 160 x 250 x 18 mm (6½ x 10 x ¾ in)
• 1 piece for base 900 x 200 x 18 mm (36 x 8 x ¾ in)

   Cut the following in planed softwood:
• 4 side supports 25 x 25 x 250 mm (1 x 1 x 10 in)
• 2 base supports 25 x 25 x 810 mm (1 x 1 x 32½ in)

2   Drill holes for screws in each corner of the side pieces and screw the side supports flush with the long edges.

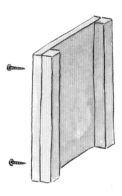

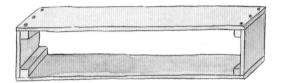

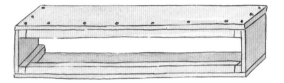

3   Drill holes along the short sides of the front and back pieces and place them flush with the outside edges of the side pieces. Screw in position.

4   Slot the base supports in between the side supports, flush with the base, and screw them in place through pre-drilled holes, front and back.

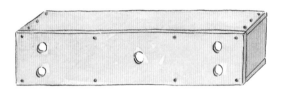

5   Drill five 25 mm (1 in) diameter drainage holes in the base, then screw the bases to the bottom of the box, driving the screws into the base supports.

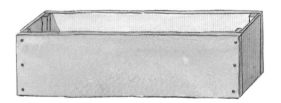

6   Coat the box inside and out with preservative. When it has completely dried, apply the green wood stain to the front, back and sides, on the outside only.

7   To decorate the front of the box, cut four sections of halved barked pole, two measuring 900 mm (36 in) and two measuring 250 mm (10 in). Mitre the ends of all four pieces, and using the 65 mm (2½ in) panel pins attach them to the front face; drive the pins in at an angle and make sure that all the corners meet.

8   For the sides, cut six sections of halved barked pole, each measuring 250 mm (10 in). Using three for each side, position the poles vertically and pin in place.

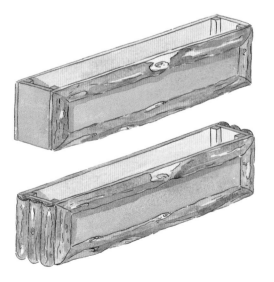

9   Cut one of the large pine cones in half lengthways with a hacksaw; use a vice to do this or pin one half of the cone to a board, which will hold the cone steady while you cut. With the tip facing downwards, pin the half-cone to the centre of the box using 50 mm (2 in) pins.

10   To complete the festoon effect, cut the small cones in half lengthways. Use a vice or construct a special cutting stand by pinning and gluing two pieces of 50 x 25 mm (2 x 1 in) timber to a plywood board, positioning them to fit the shape of the cone but leaving a gap at the top to allow for the saw. Push each cone between these rods and secure with galvanized clout nails, then cut in half with a hacksaw.

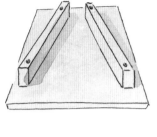

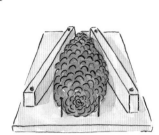

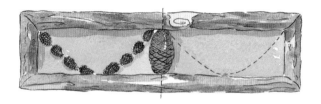

11   Draw two semicircles on each half of the front of the box as a guide for the cone festoon. Pin and glue eight half cones to each semicircle; start at the top and place matching pairs opposite one another with the tips facing downwards – if your cones are slightly different sizes, place the largest ones at the top graduating to the smallest at the central base of the festoon.

12   To construct the pine-cone finials, drill holes in the bottom of the two remaining large cones; make the holes big enough to accept half the length of the galvanized nails. Insert the nails and then cut off the heads with a hacksaw.

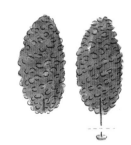

13   The finials are placed in the two side supports at the front of the box. Drill a hole for each and insert; you may want to secure them further with a dab of PVA glue.

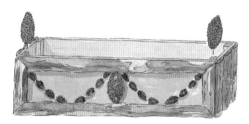

14   Line the base of the box with pot shards and half fill it with compost. Remove the plants from their pots and arrange according to the scheme below, with the larger male ferns at the back. Add compost to 25 mm (1 in) below the rim, firm in and fill any gaps with moss before watering thoroughly. Consider the positioning of the box carefully; ferns require shade and regular watering although the moss will help to retain moisture. White busy lizzies (*Impatiens*) can be used as an alternative to cup flowers.

a Versailles case

A Versailles case is a wooden box that was used at the Palace of Versailles in the 17th century for growing exotics such as oranges, lemons and palms, which could then be easily moved into the orangery and glasshouses for the winter. The great advantage of the Versailles case is that it can be unscrewed when the plants need repotting, or used as a decorative exterior for housing plants in plastic boxes or pots.

MATERIALS & EQUIPMENT

sawn timber (see step 1, page 74)

4 finials with 10 mm (½ in) diameter dowels or 4 wooden balls or pyramids with separate 10 mm (½ in) diameter dowels

square of exterior-grade plywood 375 x 375 x 10 mm (14¾ x 14¾ x ½ in)

no. 8 screws 50 mm (2 in) and 40 mm (1½ in)

glue (waterproof PVA)

1 litre (1¾ pints) wood preservative or oil-based primer

wood stain or matt emulsion paint

pot shards

50 litres moist compost

flowering tea tree (*Leptospermum scoparium*)

1 Cut the following pieces in sawn timber:

• 6 side boards 380 x 150 x 25 mm (15 x 6 x 1 in)
• 6 side boards 430 x 150 x 25 mm (17 x 6 x 1 in)
• 4 side supports 525 x 50 x 50 mm (21 x 2 x 2 in)
• 4 base supports 280 x 25 x 25 mm (11 x 1 x 1 in)

2 Prepare the shorter side boards by drilling two holes at each end 25 mm (1 in) in from the short edge, to fit the 50 mm (2 in) screws. Prepare the longer boards by drilling two holes at each end 50 mm (2 in) in from the short edge.

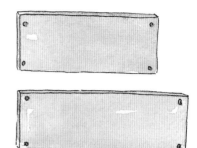

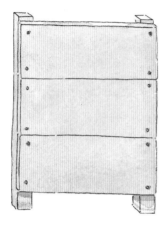

3 Using these holes, screw the shorter boards to the side supports, flush to the edge, with a 50 mm (2 in) projection at the bottom and a 25 mm (1 in) projection at the top.

4 Assemble the box shape by screwing the longer boards to the outside face of each of the side supports, creating a square-ended butt joint; use 50 mm (2 in) screws.

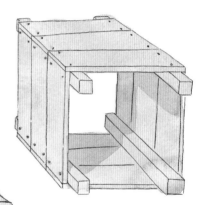

5 Prepare the base supports for 40 mm (1½ in) screws by drilling a hole about 25 mm (1 in) from each end. Place one support between each of the four side supports inside the box, positioning them at the base, flush with the bottom board. Screw in place.

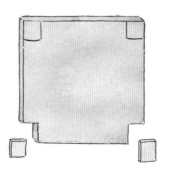

6 To fit the base, cut a 50 mm (2 in) square from each corner of the piece of plywood. Using a brace and bit, make five 25 mm (1 in) diameter drainage holes, positioning them as shown. Drop the base into the case from the top; it should rest on top of the base supports secured in the previous step.

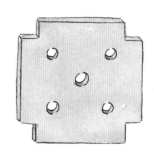

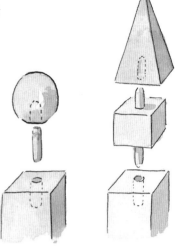

7 To attach the finials, drill a 10 mm (½ in) diameter hole for the dowel in the top of each upright, positioning it centrally. Use waterproof PVA glue to secure the finial in the prepared hole.

Alternatively make your own finials, fixing them in place as above on a separate 50 mm (2 in) long dowel. Suitable designs for this size of case include a 50 mm (2 in) diameter wooden ball, or a 130 mm (5 in) high pyramid cut from a 50 x 50 mm (2 x 2 in) rod and sitting on a 25 x 30 x 30 mm (1 x 1¼ x 1¼ in) block.

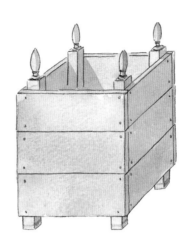

8 To protect the case, coat it in wood preservative inside and out. Then apply a wood stain or paint. Make sure the paint is thoroughly dry before planting up.

9 Line the base of the case with pot shards and enough moist compost so that the top of the potted plant sits 40 mm (1½ in) from the top of the container. Remove the plant from its pot and tease out the roots. Place inside the case and fill the surrounding space with the remaining compost to within 40 mm (1½ in) of the top. Firm loosely and keep well watered.

A flowering tea tree has been used here, but Versailles cases are suitable for large shrubs, topiary and masses of summer bedding.

10 After the tree has flowered, trim the outer leaves to keep the circular ball shape.

a wood and trellis camouflage box

This container is designed to mask plants in plastic pots for seasonally changing arrangements. There is no base – simply fit it over your potted plants, enclosing the display within a decorated wooden case. A useful disguise for unattractive pots, this box also enables you to mix plant varieties that have different soil and feeding requirements.

MATERIALS & EQUIPMENT

2 pieces exterior-grade plywood 600 x 380 x 18 mm (24 x 15 x ¾ in)

2 pieces exterior-grade plywood 560 x 380 x 18 mm (22½ x 15 x ¾ in)

4 pieces planed softwood 750 x 50 x 50 mm (30 x 2 x 2 in)

13.6 m (44 ft) length of 25 x 10 mm (1 x 1½ in) planed softwood for trellis

1 litre (1¾ pints) each clear wood preservative and matt emulsion paint

sheradized panel pins 50 mm (2 in) and 25 mm (1 in)

glue (waterproof PVA)

no. 8 screws, 50 mm (2 in)

16 standard sized bricks

4 marguerites (*Argyranthemum frutescens*) in

250 mm (10 in) diameter plastic pots

1   To assemble the sides of the box, place the ends of the shorter boards against the inside face of the longer ones; glue in place, then reinforce with panel pins. Mark a line 50 mm (2 in) from the top all the way around the box; the trellis will be fixed below this line.

To apply the trellis to the outside of the box, follow steps 2, 3, 4 and 5 for each of the four sides.

2   Measure and cut a length of trellis to form a diagonal strut. Lay it against the side of the box with its centre line on the centre line of the diagonal. Mark and mitre the ends to match the corners of the box. Repeat for the other diagonal but cut a piece from the middle of the strut to fit. Glue and pin with panel pins.

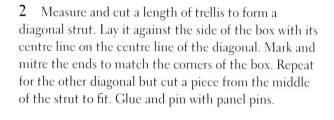

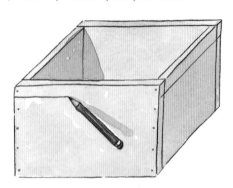

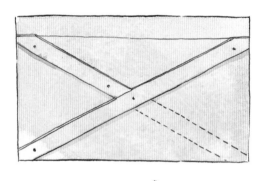

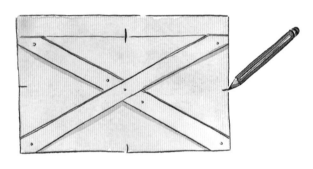

3   Use a pencil to mark the centre points of each side at the edges. These marks will serve as guides for the accurate construction of the central lozenge shape.

4   Make the first of the four lozenge struts by placing a section of trellis in a line from a top or bottom centre mark to a side mark. Cut a piece from the middle of this strut so that it fits around the latticework already in place, and mitre the ends.

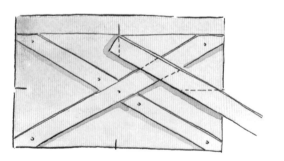

5   Repeat step 4 for the other lozenge struts and fit them together on the box, matching the mitred ends. Pin and glue in place.

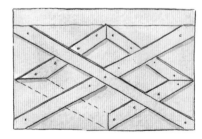

6   Treat the wood and trellis box inside and out with clear preservative and allow it to dry.

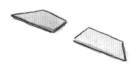

7   To form the top moulding, mitre the ends of the four pieces of pre-cut softwood so that they fit together snugly around the top edge of the box.

8 Prepare the box for the moulding by drilling holes for the screws along the top edges. Screw the moulding to the box from the inside so that it lies flush with the top edges. Reinforce the mitred corners with panel pins.

9 Apply two coats of matt emulsion in the colour of your choice to the inside and outside of the box.

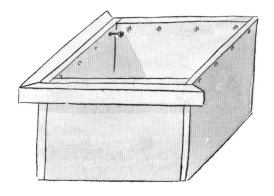

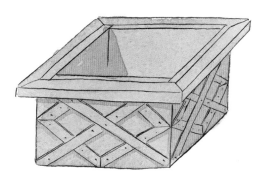

10 You may need to raise a platform to ensure that the tops of the pots rest just below the top of the moulding. In this project four bricks have been placed under each of the pots so that they sit 10 mm (½ in) below the top edge of the container; leave small gaps between the bricks to allow for drainage.

11 Place the plastic pots inside the container, one on each block of bricks. Marguerites have been picked for this display because their mass of foliage and flowers works well with the proportions of the box.

alternative planting schemes

4 *Fuchsia* x *speciosa* 'La Bianca'; 4 *Daphne odorata* 'Aureomarginata'; 4 common ivy (*Hedera helix* 'Erecta') around a common box (*Buxus sempervirens*); 4 bear's breeches (*Acanthus mollis*); 4 *Camellia japonica*.

a trough with trellis screen

This versatile trellis-backed trough is essentially a portable container for tall
plants and climbers and can be moved whenever you want to change your garden layout.
It acts as both a screen and a planter and is ideal for use on a balcony or roof garden
where it may be difficult to support posts.

MATERIALS & EQUIPMENT

sawn timber (see step 1, opposite)

no. 8 screws 40 mm (1½ in), 65 mm (2½ in) and 100 mm (4 in)

sheradized panel pins 40 mm (1½ in)

1 piece exterior-grade plywood 845 x 345 x 20 mm (33¾ x 13¾ x ¾ in)

13.7 m (45 ft) length of planed softwood for trellis 30 x 20 mm (1¼ x ¾ in)

1 litre (1¾ pints) wood preservative and 2½ litres (4½ pints) wood stain

pot shards

50 litres compost

1 *Trachelospermum jasminoides*

2 lesser periwinkles (*Vinca minor*)

3 sky-blue lesser periwinkles (*Vinca minor* 'Azurea Flore Plena')

10 *Petunia* 'Dark Blue Dwarf'

1   Cut the following pieces in sawn timber:
• 4 pieces for sides 350 x 150 x 25 mm (14 x 6 x 1 in)
• 4 pieces for front and back 900 x 150 x 25 mm
(36 x 6 x 1 in)
• 4 side supports 300 x 50 x 50 mm (12 x 2 x 2 in)
• 2 base supports 750 x 25 x 25 mm (30 x 1 x 1 in)
• 2 base supports 250 x 25 x 25 mm (10 x 1 x 1 in)
• 2 trellis supports 1700 x 50 x 50 mm (68 x 2 x 2 in)

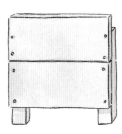

2   Drill holes for 50 mm (2 in) screws at both ends of the side boards. Use two boards for each side and screw them to the side supports, lining up the outer edges and staggering them so that two 50 mm (2 in) legs protrude from the bottom.

3   Assemble the box by screwing the front and back boards to the outside face of the sides; drill holes and use 50 mm (2 in) screws to secure the joint.

4   Drill the base supports for the 40 mm (1½ in) screws and slot the base supports between the side supports on the inside, flush with the base. Secure them in place with screws.

5   For the base, cut a 50 x 50 mm (2 x 2 in) square from each corner of the piece of plywood. Before dropping the plywood over the base supports, drill five 25 mm (1 in) diameter drainage holes.

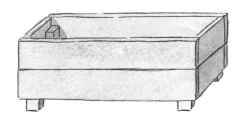

6   Treat the box and base with clear wood preservative. When it has dried, apply a couple of coats of stain.

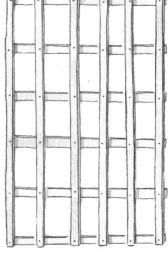

7   To make the trellis panel, cut the planed softwood into six sections measuring 1.35 m (54 in) and six measuring 900 mm (36 in). Start by making a rectangular frame: pin two of the shorter sections behind the longer ones, flush with the ends.

8   Divide each side into five equal parts and mark the divisions with a pencil. Pin the vertical sections of trellis first, top and bottom, and then the horizontals behind these, pinning at all junctions. Treat the structure and the trellis supports with clear wood preservative.

9   Drill the trellis supports for 65 mm (2½ in) and place them against the back of the trellis, flush with the top and sides. Screw in place from the front. Stain the trellis and supports.

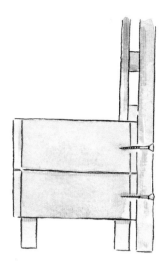

10   To join trough and trellis, drill holes in the trellis supports for 100 mm (4 in) screws; position the holes so that the screws will go through the trellis and the side supports inside the trough. Make sure that all sides and bottom edges line up and screw the pieces together.

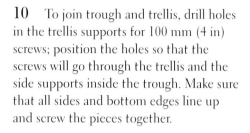

11   Line the trough with pot shards and enough compost to ensure that the top of the plant sits about 25 mm (1 in) from the top edge. It is advisable to use a tall trained trachelospermum for this project; if your plants are small, it may be better to use two.

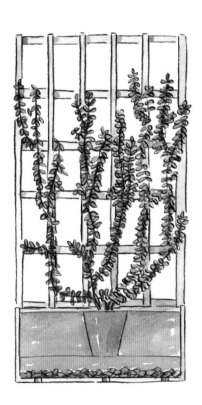

12   Place the plant in the centre at the back of the trough, tease out the individual stems and arrange them on the front of the trellis as evenly as possible; tie them to the trellis with coated wire.

13   Place the lesser periwinkles along the length of the trough and fill in the spaces with dark blue petunias. Add potting compost as you go, then firm in and water the trough. Use a liquid feed about once a fortnight.

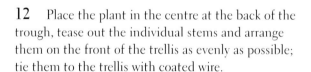

alternative planting scheme

For a colder climate, plant the semi-evergreen wall shrub *Pyracantha coccinea*, underplanted with *Hedera helix*. For the trellis backing you could also use a more hedge-like plant such as a hawthorn or holly or even the much despised *Aucuba japonica*, which thrives even in very polluted environments.

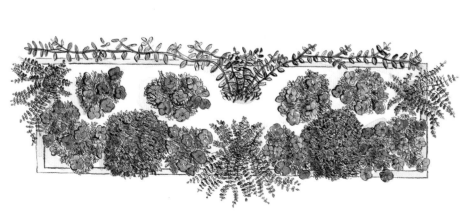

planted entrance containers

It is often useful to be able to raise plants high up so that they can be appreciated
from a distance. Use the planters in pairs to resemble gateposts or as part of a screen to mark
a division in the garden. These wooden gate piers have been designed as cachepots so the
individual plants remain in their plastic pots and can be changed seasonally.

MATERIALS & EQUIPMENT

1 sheet exterior-grade plywood 2400 x 1200 x 12 mm (96 x 48 x ½ in)

2 squares exterior-grade plywood 290 x 290 x 12 mm (11½ x 11½ x ½ in)

sawn timber or planed softwood (see steps 2, 3, 5, 6, opposite)

exterior-grade wood preservative or oil-based primer

2½ litres (4½ pints) matt emulsion or microporous paint

glue (waterproof PVA)

sheradized panel pins 50 mm (2 in)

galvanized clout nails 40 mm (1½ in)

no. 8 screws 30 mm (1¼ in) and 75 mm (3 in)

4 *Hydrangea macrophylla*

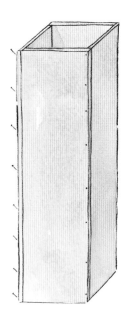

1   Cut the sheet of exterior-grade plywood into eight equal pieces, each measuring 1200 x 300 mm (48 x 12 in). Using square-ended butt joints, make two boxes by gluing the end of each board to the inside face of another; use panel pins inserted at a slight angle.

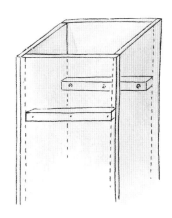

2   For the base supports cut four battens in sawn timber, each measuring 290 x 25 x 25 mm (11½ x 1 x 1 in). Position two battens on the inside of each box, opposite one another and 230 mm (9 in) down from the top. Drill holes in the plywood for 30 mm (1¼ in) screws. Glue the battens in place and secure with screws in the holes.

3   To make the top mouldings cut four pieces of sawn timber for each pier, 410 x 50 x 50 mm (16½ x 2 x 2 in). Mitre the corners to fit around the top outside edges. Glue and nail the mouldings in place flush with the top edge and finish by reinforcing the mitred corners with panel pins.

4   Treat the gate piers inside and out with clear wood preservative, making sure you coat the base thoroughly. When it has dried, apply two coats of matt emulsion or microporous paint to the outside and the inside down to the level of the base supports.

If the pier planters are to be placed on soil, follow step 5. To fix them to concrete or paving, follow step 6.

5   Make eight supporting stakes from sawn timber, each measuring 450 x 30 x 30 mm (18 x 1½ x 1½ in); sharpen one end on each until it forms a point. For each pier, knock four stakes into the soil, spacing them to fit into the inside corners; the internal dimensions of the pier are 290 mm (11½ in) square. Leave at least 150 mm (6 in) of stake above the soil. Lower each pier over the stakes to sit on the ground and check that the structure is vertical – a spirit level is useful here). If the surface is uneven, bank it up with soil so that the tops of both piers are level. Drill holes for 30 mm (1¼ in) screws in the bottom corners of the pier and then screw the stakes to the plywood structure.

6 To fix the pier to concrete, cut four battens from sawn timber, each measuring 290 x 50 x 50 mm (11½ x 2 x 2 in). Using two for each pier, place them opposite one another with the outside edges 290 mm (11½ in) apart. Rawlplug them for 75 mm (3 in) screws and, using a hammer drill with a masonry bit, secure them to the concrete. Slot the pier over the battens. Check they are level. Drill holes for 30 mm (1¼ in) screws and screw the pier to the battens through the sides.

7 Make the base to hold the plants from the remaining squares of plywood. Drill five 25 mm (1 in) diameter holes through them for drainage purposes. Treat both squares with clear wood preservative before dropping them onto the supporting battens inside each pier.

8 The piers are now ready to be planted by placing the plastic container directly onto the wooden stage. Hydrangeas have been used for this project, but the height of the base and pier can be adjusted to suit plants of different size and shape.

alternative planting scheme

Other suitable plants for this arrangement include a box ball (*Buxus sempervirens*) or marguerites (*Argyranthemum frutescens*). You can adjust the height of the base and pier to suit the size and shape of your chosen plant. Keep all plants fed and watered according to their individual needs.

a wooden obelisk

Trellis obelisks have long been used as a decorative element in the garden.
They create an attractive feature on their own, or in pairs frame a view or emphasize
a formal approach to a house. The shape of the obelisk makes it suitable for supporting
climbers such as ivy, clematis, honeysuckle and hops. In this project, quick-growing
hawthorn has been used; as the hawthorn spreads, use the trellis as a clipping
guide to create a tall, elegant pyramid shape.

MATERIALS & EQUIPMENT

sawn timber (see steps 1, 2, 5 and 6, page 90)

square of exterior-grade plywood 380 x 380 x 12 mm (15 x 15 x ½ in)

no. 8 screws 40 mm (1½ in) and 50 mm (2 in)

sheradized panel pins 40 mm (1½ in)

1 litre (1¾ pints) clear wood preservative or oil-based primer

1 litre (1¾ pints) wood stain

50 litres potting compost

pot shards

4 bare-root hawthorns (*Crataegeus monogyna*)

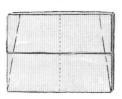 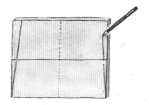

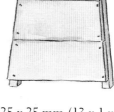

1   For each of the two short and two long sides of the tub, put together two 150 mm (6 in) wide timber boards. For the short sides, measure and mark the bottom length of 390 mm (15 in), draw a vertical line through its centre, then measure out the top length of 340 mm (13½ in) extending equally on each side of this line. Use these marks to draw the tapered sides before cutting out. Repeat for the two longer sides, measuring 430 mm (17 in) along the bottom and 380 mm (15 in) along the top.

2   Take the two shorter sides and drill holes for the 40 mm (1½ in) screws, 10 mm (½ in) in from the tapered edges. Cut four corner supports in sawn timber, each measuring 330 x 25 x 25 mm (13 x 1 x 1 in), and position flush with the pre-drilled sides and top, leaving a 25 mm (1 in) projection at the bottom. Screw in place.

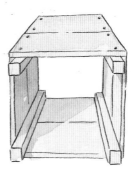

3   Position the longer sides against the outside face of the shorter ones, for a square-ended butt joint. Screw in place, making the holes 40 mm (1½ in) in from the sides of the longer pieces.

4   For the base, take the piece of plywood and cut a 25 x 25 mm (1 x 1 in) square from each corner. Drill five 25 mm (1 in) diameter drainage holes, positioning as shown. Insert the base in position from the bottom of the tub before attaching the four base supports.

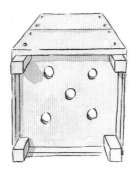

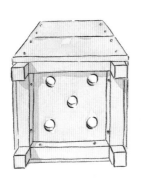

5   Cut four base supports 340 x 25 x 25 mm (13½ x 1 x 1 in) in sawn timber and position flush with the bottom edge of the container on all four sides. Secure with 40 mm (1½ in) screws in pre-drilled holes.

6   For the obelisk, cut the following pieces in sawn timber:

• 4 side supports 2350 x 25 x 25 mm (90 x 1 x 1 in)
• 18 m (60 ft) of 25 x 20 mm (1 x 1¾ in) cut into lengths for rungs
• 1 block 100 x 100 x 100 mm (4 x 4 x 4 in) to form tapered top
• 1 board 100 x 100 x 25 mm (4 x 4 x 1 in) to form base of top

7   Place two side supports 100 mm (4 in) apart at the top and 480 mm (19 in) apart at the bottom. Cut and position one rung 130 mm (5 in) from the top and one 150 mm (6 in) from the bottom as shown – make the rungs slightly longer than the actual width. Fix in place with panel pins. Mark the positions of 14 rungs between them at 140 mm (5½ in) intervals. Repeat for the opposite side.

8   Cut and pin 14 rungs to the marked positions then cut off all overhangs flush with the side supports.

9 To assemble the obelisk, lay the two completed sections on their sides and cut and pin a top and bottom rung in place across them, positioning as in step 7. Mark the positions of the rest of the rungs as before then cut and pin them, making sure they line up on all sides. Repeat for the fourth side and cut off the overhangs.

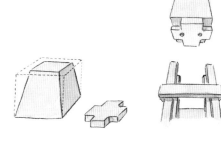

10 For the top, taper the block at an 85° angle. Then cut four 25 x 25 mm (1 x 1 in) squares from the corners of the board. Drill holes in this board and screw to the wide base of the top piece using the 50 mm (2 in) long screws. Slot on top of the main structure and pin to the side supports.

11 Before assembling the whole structure, treat the obelisk and tub with wood preservative. When the surface is dry, apply two coats of coloured wood stain.

12 Plant the tub with four bare-root hawthorns. Line the bottom with pot shards and place the root balls on potting compost, leaning them slightly towards the centre. Fill the tub to within 25 mm (1 in) of the top edge.

13 To join the tub and obelisk, first cut four battens 400 x 25 x 25 mm (16 x 1 x 1 in). Drill them for 40 mm (1½ in) screws and fix two each to opposite sides of the tub; place one flush with the top and the other 130 mm (5 in) below it.

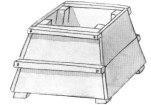

14 Fit the obelisk over the tub, making sure that the structure is square, and screw as above, fixing the bottom two rungs to the battens on the sides of the tub.

15 Make sure the tub is well watered and use a liquid feed during the growing season. Use the trellis as a guide to clipping the hawthorn so that a tall slender green pyramid is achieved. Hawthorn may need clipping several times a year.

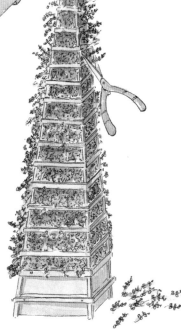

a primula theatre

This design for a primula theatre is for a scaled-down version of an early 19th-century
type of shaded staging, made to show off the best examples in a collection and to protect
the flowers from sun and rain. It will comfortably hold up to fifteen 100 mm (4 in) pots;
terracotta pots look best. Paint or stain the theatre dark blue, dark green, grey or black
to form a good background for the rich and varied colours of the primulas.

MATERIALS & EQUIPMENT

planed softwood or sawn timber (see steps, opposite)

shuttering or other exterior-grade plywood (see steps, opposite)

1 litre (1¾ pints) wood preservative or oil-based primer

sheradized nails and panel pins

glue (waterproof PVA)

microporous paint or wood stain

13 terracotta pots with 100 mm (4 in) diameters

Primula vulgaris

P. denticulata

P. veris

P. Gold Lace Group

*Please note: This project is fairly complex. If you do not
have good carpentry skills, you may want to consult a professional.*

1   Cut the wood according to the diagrams and measurements.

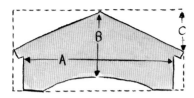

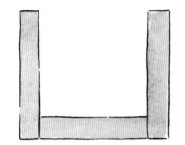

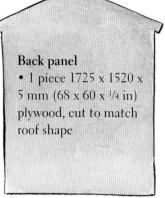

front elevation
- 1 top piece 1520 x 560 x 12 mm
  (60 x 22 x ½ in) plywood
  A: 1395 mm (55 in)
  B: 540 mm (21¼ in)
  C: 200 mm (8 in)
- 2 pieces 1110 x 150 x 25 mm (43¾ x 6 x 1 in)
  planed softwood
- 1 bottom piece 1095 x 180 x 25 mm
  (43 x 7 x 1 in) plywood

Back panel
- 1 piece 1725 x 1520 x
  5 mm (68 x 60 x ¼ in)
  plywood, cut to match
  roof shape

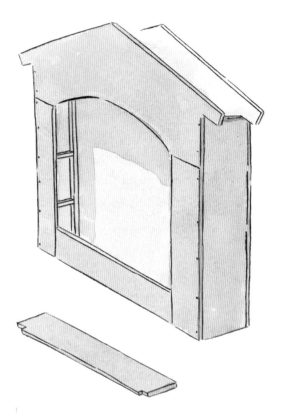

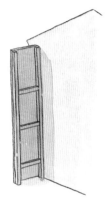

sides and supports
- 2 side panels 1395 x 200 x 12 mm
  (55 x 8 x ½ in) plywood
- 4 side supports 1395 x 25 x 25 mm
  (55 x 1 x 1 in) planed softwood
- 6 shelf supports 150 x 25 x 25 mm
  (6 x 1 x 1 in) planed softwood

2   To make up the sides, glue and nail the side supports to the outer edges of the two side panels. Then pin and glue the shelf supports 150, 480 and 785 mm (6, 19 and 31 in) from the bottom of the side panels. Now glue and pin both completed sides to the plywood back.

3   Construct the carcass by attaching the front elevation to the back and sides, pinning and gluing throughout.

4   Cut all the shelves but only attach the bottom one at this stage; sit it on the bottom side supports and pin and glue to the edge of the front elevation.

shelves
- 2 pieces 1370 x 150 x 25 mm
  (54 x 6 x 1 in) planed softwood
- 1 bottom piece 1395 x 180 x 25 mm
  (55 x 7 x 1 in) planed softwood with
  two 25 x 25 mm (1 x 1 in) notches cut
  from both corners on one long side

5   Secure the roof supports as shown. Wipe off any excess glue. (The actual roof goes on last.)

roof supports
- 6 roof supports
  200 x 50 x 50 mm
  (8 x 2 x 2 in)
  planed softwood

6 Cut out the upper and lower sections of the top pediment from softwood. Secure mitred edges with glue, reinforcing with panel pins. Glue and nail to the carcass in the positions indicated – place the upper section first.

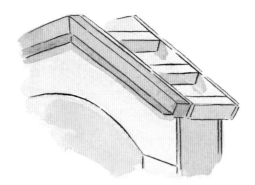

top pediment
- 2 upper sections 50 x 50 mm (2 x 2 in) approximately 760 mm (30 in) long to fit the size of the pediment, mitred at one end
- 2 lower sections 25 x 25 mm (1 x 1 in) approximately 760 mm (30 in) long to fit the size of the pediment, mitred at both ends

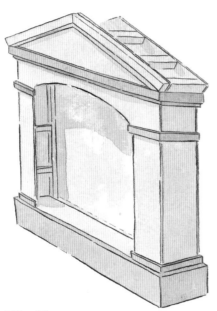

7 Using softwood cut out the base pediment, the capitals, the base column and the skirting, as highlighted in the diagram, from top to bottom. Secure in the same way as for the top pediment (see step 6).

base pediment
- 1 upper section 1495 x 50 x 50 mm (59 x 2 x 2 in) mitred at both ends
- 2 upper side sections 280 x 50 x 50 mm (11¼ x 2 x 2 in) mitred at one end
- 1 lower section 1445 x 25 x 25 mm (57 x 1 x 1 in) mitred at both ends
- 2 lower side sections 260 x 25 x 25 mm (10¼ x 1 x 1 in) mitred at one end

capitals
All pieces to be mitred at one end.
- 2 pieces 245 x 25 x 25 mm (9¾ x 1 x 1 in)
- 2 pieces 200 x 25 x 25 mm (8 x 1 x 1 in)

base column
All pieces to be mitred at one end.
- 2 pieces 245 x 10 x 25 mm (9¾ x ½ x 1 in)
- 2 pieces 180 x 10 x 25 mm (7 x ½ x 1 in)

skirting
- 1 piece 1445 x 180 x 25mm (57 x 7 x 1 in) mitred at both ends
- 2 pieces 260 x 180 x 25 mm (10¼ x 7 x 1 in) mitred at one end

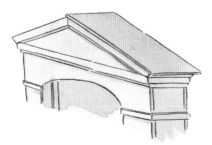

8 Cut out the roof pieces and nail in place, lining up the back edge with the back panel.

- 2 pieces 780 x 305 x 10 mm (30¾ x 12 x ½ in) plywood, mitred at one end

9 Treat the theatre and shelves with a suitable wood preservative. Finish by painting with a microporous paint or an exterior decorative wood stain. Make sure that the staging is thoroughly dry and aired before placing plants, since preservatives and stains are often toxic to plants. Insert the two remaining shelves. Choose your plants from the selection listed. Plant them in shallow terracotta pots lined with pot shards and display on the staged shelving.

plant directory

key

H *height*

S *spread*

● *fully hardy: -15°C (5°F) and below*

❖ *frost hardy: down to -5°C (23°F)*

❱ *half hardy: down to 0°C (32°F)*

T *tender: down to 10–18°C (52–66°F)*

Acanthus mollis (Bear's breeches)
H: 90–120 cm (3–4ft); S: 120 cm (4 ft) ●
Herbaceous perennial with large
beautifully shaped leaves, much used in
classical ornamentation. White or pink
flowers come in July to August on 45 cm
(18 in) long spikes. Prefers full sun.

Agapanthus africanus
'Headbourne Hybrids'
H: 1 m (3 ft); S: 50 cm (20 in) ❱
Late summer flowering perennial.
Deep blue-violet bell-shaped flowers
and long evergreen leaves. Plant in
well-drained soil in sun or light shade.
Cover in winter or keep in a greenhouse.

Ageratum houstonianum 'Blue Danube'
H and S: 15 cm (6 in) ❱
Summer flowering annual with blue,
purple and pink heart-shaped flowers. Sow
in a warm greenhouse and plant out late.

Anthemis nobile 'Treneague'
(Lawn chamomile)
H: 2.5 cm (1 in); S: 45 cm (18 in) ●
Moss-like carpet of grass with aromatic
finely divided leaves; non-flowering. Plant
in a well-drained and sunny place.

Aptenia cordifolia 'Variegata'
H: 5 cm (2 in); S: indefinite
Low-growing perennial succulent.
Bright green leaves with cream edges
and small daisy-like blue and pink
flowers in summer. Requires full sun
and well-drained soil.

Artemesia 'Powys Castle'
H: 60–90 cm (24–36 in); S: 1.2 m (4 ft)❖
Perennial dwarf, non-flowering silver-
leaved variety will thrive in well-drained
compost and full sun. Can be clipped back
in spring to keep compact shape.

Aster (Michaelmas daisy)
A genus of perennials and deciduous or
evergreen sub-shrubs that like well-drained
soil and a sunny aspect. Characterized
by daisy-like flower heads.

A. novae-belgii 'Audrey'
H and S: 30 cm (12 in) ●
Pale blue, semi-double pointed flowers
that open up in autumn.

A. novae-belgii 'Snowsprite'
H and S: 30 cm (12 in) ●
White slender-pointed flowers in autumn.

Athyrium filix-femina cristatum
(Crested female fern)
H and S: 90 cm (3 ft) ●
Fern with tall lacy fresh green crested
fronds. Water freely March to October.
Minutissimum is a miniature form of the
female fern only 10–15 cm (4–6 in) high.

Aucuba japonica 'Crotonifolia'
H: 1.8–2.7 m (6–9 ft) ●
Evergreen shrub best grown in shade.
The speckled yellow and green leaves
withstand urban pollution. 'Borealis' is
a dwarf green variety.

Buxus sempervirens

Calendula officinalis

Chrysanthemum frutescens

Aurinia saxatalis
(syn. ***Alyssum saxatile***)
H: 23 cm (9 in); S: 30 cm (12 in) ●
Sub-shrub with grey foliage and light
yellow clusters of flowers. Likes full sun.
Cut back after flowering.

Buxus sempervirens (Common box)
H: up to 4.5 m (15 ft) ●
Medium-sized evergreen shrub or small
tree that thrives in sun or shade. Usually
used for dwarf hedges or for topiary.
Produces luxurious masses of small dark
evergreen leaves. Trim after growth in
summer to maintain a uniform shape.

Calendula officinalis (Pot marigold)
H and S: 50–70 cm (20–28 in) ●
Annual with yellow to orange flowers in
summer and autumn. Likes well-drained
soil and full sun. Self-seeds.

Camellia japonica (Common camellia)
H: up to 9 m (30 ft) ●
Evergreen lime-hating shrub or small tree
with large flowers in varying colours in
early spring. Will grow up to 1.8 m (6 ft)
in a large tub. Acid to neutral peaty soil
works best, prefers a lightly shaded
position. 'Mathotiana Alba' is a good
white double variety.

Campanula carpatica (Bell flower)
H: 8–10 cm (3–4 in); S: 30 cm (12 in)●
Rock perennial with blue, mauve or
lavender-blue flowers, either solitary
or several to a stem. Flowers freely in
summer in an open or semi-shaded
position and well-drained soil.

Chaenomeles japonica 'Alba'
H: 1–3.7 m (3–12 ft) ●
Deciduous shrub with early spring
flowers – these ones have white flowers.
This plant will happily grow in a shaded
environment. It is advisable to cut
back immediately after flowering in
order to keep the shape compact.

Chrysanthemum frutescens
(syn. ***Argyranthemum frutescens***)
(Marguerite)
H and S: 1 m (3 ft) T
Shrubby perennial with greyish foliage
and white or yellow daisy-like flowers
with yellow centres. Flowers over a long
summer period if dead-headed. Train
as a standard or tight ball by pinching
out the foliage ends. Do not put out
until the end of May.

Citrus limon 'Meyer'
H: 45–60 cm (18–24 in); S: 45–50 cm
(18–20 in) ❖
Evergreen medium to large shrub with
large bright green leaves and heavily
scented white flowers in spring and
summer followed by large lemons;
flowers and fruits together. Overwinter
in a greenhouse or conservatory but
may be put outside after frosts, in
a sheltered sunny place. Keep well
watered in summer months.

Convolvulus sabatius
(syn. ***C. mauritanicus***)
H: 15–20 cm (6–8 in); S: 30 cm (12 in) ▶
Rock trailing perennial with blue-mauve
flowers.

Coreopsis tincturia (Tickseed)
H: 60–90 cm (2–3 ft); S: 20 cm (8 in) ▶
Annual with yellow to crimson brown-
edged flowers in summer. Also coloured
hybrids.

Cordyline indivisa
(syn. ***Dracaena indivisa***)
H: 3 m (10 ft); S: 2 m (6 ft) T
Evergreen tree or shrub with long spiky
leaves – grey with red or yellow stripe.

Crataegus monogyna

Delphinium Belladonna 'Wendy'

Fuchsia x *speciosa* 'La Bianca'

Crataegus monogyna (Common hawthorn)
H: up to 6 m (20 ft) ●
Quick-growing deciduous small tree. White flowers and red fruit and autumn foliage. Excellent for quick topiary; clip throughout the growing season.

Cyclamen
A genus of tuberous perennials with pendulous flowers and five reflexed petals. Likes a sunny aspect and well-drained soil.
C. cilicium
H: 10 cm (4 in); S: 5–10 cm (2–4 in) ●
Roundish leaves with silvery markings and pale pink flowers in autumn.
C. hederifolium
H: 10 cm (4 in); S: 5–10 cm (2–4 in) ▶
Ivy-shaped leaves with scented pink flowers in autumn, from September to October.

Daphne odora 'Aureomarginata'
H and S: 1.5 m (5 ft) ▶
Dwarf evergreen spreading shrub. Narrow leaves have a yellow margin and the white flowers are very fragrant. Place in a sunny sheltered position.

Delphinium Belladonna 'Wendy'
H: 60 cm (24 in); S: 20 cm (8 in) ●
Perennial with gentian blue flowers in summer. Also available in pale blue, white and pink.

Dryopteris filix-mas (Male fern)
H and S: 40 cm (16 in) ●
Deciduous or semi-evergreen bright green fern. Needs shade and humus-rich compost. Keep moist.

Exacum affine (Persian violet)
H: 15 cm (6 in) T
Perennial with bluish lilac fragrant flowers in June to October. Water freely and overwinter indoors.

Festuca glauca (Blue fescue)
H and S: 9 in (23 cm)
Perennial thin-leaved grass forms bright blue to grey dense tufts. At its best in the sun from spring to midsummer.

Fuchsia
Genus of deciduous shrubs with pendulous bell-shaped flowers. Plant in a sunny place and cover roots with mulch.
F. 'Margaret'
H: 1 m (3 ft); S: 75 cm (2½ ft) T
Vigorous shrub. Crimson and violet-purple semi-double flowers.

F. x speciosa 'La Bianca'
H and S: 60 cm (2 ft) T
Hybrid shrub. Flowers are pink. Overwinter in a cool greenhouse, put out in May. Train as a half or full standard.

Gazania 'Orange Beauty'
H and S: 30 cm (12 in) ▶
Perennial that displays brilliant orange flowers from late June and has silver-grey foliage. Plant in late May in light sandy compost in the sun. Protect from frost. A variety of colours is available.

Hebe pinguifolia 'Pagei'
H: 15–30 cm (6–12 in); S: 60–100 cm (2–3 ft)❖
Dwarf evergreen grey-leaved shrub. Forms very satisfactory grey foliage mounds. White flowers in late spring.

Hedera (Ivy)
A genus of evergreen woody-stemmed, trailing perennials with green or variegated lobed leaves. Prefers well-drained soil.
H. helix (Common English ivy)
H and S: up to 3 m (10 ft)
Climbing or trailing evergreen, also 'self branching'. Can be trained over frames. Other varieties include *H. helix* 'Glacier', *H. helix* 'Autropureum' and *H. helix* 'Adam'.

Helianthus 'Lodden Gold'

Heliotropium peruvianum 'Royal Marine'

Hydrangea macrophylla 'Blue Wave'

H. helix 'Erecta' (Upright ivy)
H: 10 m (30 ft); S: 5 m (15 ft)
Upright form of *Hedera helix*. Useful
clipped in window boxes as an
alternative to box or as a year-round
support structure for seasonal planting.

Helianthus 'Loddon Gold' (Sunflower)
H: 1.2–1.5 m (4–5 ft) ●
Annual with double golden yellow
flowers in July to September. Needs sun.

Heliotropium peruvianum 'Royal
Marine' (Heliotrope, Cherry Pie)
H: 38–90 cm (15–36 in); S: 30–38 cm
(12–15 in) ◗
This purplish green-leaved perennial has
heavily scented deep violet blue flowers.
Needs to be planted in a sunny position
in early June. Overwinter in a cool
greenhouse or conservatory. Can be
trained as a standard on a cane.

Holcus mollis 'Albovariegatus'
(Creeping softgrass)
H: 30–45 cm (12–18 in); S: indefinite ●
Evergreen, spreading perennial grass
with white-and-green varigated foliage.
In summer it carries purplish-white
flower spikes.

Hosta
A genus of herbaceous perennials grown
for abundant foliage ranging from blues
to silver-green and golden colours. Will
tolerate shade and prefers damp soil.
H. fortunei var. **aureomarginata**
H: 60 cm (2 ft) ●
Leaves are edged in yellow and late
spring flowers are lilac.
H. sieboldiana var. **elegans**
H: 60–90 cm (2–3 ft) ●
Bold blue-green foliage and violet
flowers in early summer.

Hyacinthus orientalis 'Delft Blue'
H: 25 cm (10 in); S: 15 cm (6 in) ●
Pale blue heavily scented flowers
produced from a bulb in April. Plant
from mid-September. Water well
when growing. Other colours and
dwarf varieties available.

Hydrangea macrophylla 'Blue Wave'
(Lace-cap hydrangea)
H: up to 1.8 m (6 ft) ●
Deciduous shrub, has dense heads
of variable blue flowers in summer.
Flowers change to pink in alkaline
soils. Add aluminium sulphate to
change back to blue.

Ilex (Holly)
Evergreen deciduous trees or shrubs
with glossy green foliage and berries.
Tolerates sun and shade. Prefers to be
planted in well-drained soil.
I. x meserveae 'Blue Prince'
H: up to 3 m (10 ft) ●
Vigorous growth of dark blue-green
foliage.
I. aquifolium 'Silver Queen'
H: 5 m (20 ft); S: 4 m (12 ft) ●
Variegated leaves of green mottled grey
with white margins and reddish stems
and no berries. Often grown as a standard.
Clips well into dense formal shape.
Despite its name, it is a male plant.
I. crenata
H: 5 m (15 ft); S: 3 m (10 ft) ●
Tiny box-like dark green leaves. Keeps a
compact shape when pruned.

Impatiens balsamina (Busy Lizzy)
H: 23 cm (9 in) ◗
Annuals available in wide range of
colours with both double and single
flowers. Place in a sheltered sunny
position in rich moist compost.

Leptospermum scoparium

Lilium 'Reinesse'

Myosotis alpestris

Laurentia axialaris 'Blue Star'
H: 15 cm (6 in) ▶
Small-growing annual related to lobelia.
Pale blue-mauve flowers from June
onwards and light green foliage. Plant
in full sun in well-drained soil.

Leptospermum scoparium (Tea tree)
H: up to 3 m (10 ft) T
Evergreen shrub with dark greyish green
leaves and small pink flowers that begin
in early summer and continue over a long
period. Overwinter in a cool greenhouse.
Good flowering topiary subject.

Lilium 'Reinesse'
H: 30 cm (12 in) ●
Bulb produces pale yellow or white flowers
in summer. Likes well-drained soil. Dead-
head and keep out of direct sun.

Linaria cymbalaria (Ivy-leaved toadflax)
H: 10–15 cm (4–6 in) ●
Trailing perennial with lilac flowers in
summer. Good in hanging baskets.
Water freely in summer and keep virtually
dry in winter.

Lobelia erinus 'Pendula Blue Cascade'
H: 10–20 cm (4–8 in); S: 10–15 cm (4–6 in) ▶
Trailing annual. Light blue flowers in
summer, good in hanging baskets.

Morus alba 'Pendula' (Weeping
mulberry)
H: 1.8–2.5 m (6–8 ft) ●
Deciduous tree with attractive weeping
foliage and mulberry fruit. Protect from
strong winds. Prune in February, thinning
overcrowded branches. Plant from
October to March.

Myosotis alpestris (Forget-me-not)
H and S: 15–23 cm (6–9 in) ●
Biennial or perennial. Pot up early
autumn. Pale blue flowers appear in mid-
spring to early summer. A beautiful
feathery underplanting for tulips.
Available in white and various dark blues.

Nemesia caerulea
H: 25 cm (10 in) ▶
Annual, plant out in June in sun.
Propagate by seed sown in March.

Nicotiana (Tobacco plant)
Genus of perennials treated as annuals
with tubular scented flowers. Plant in
well-drained soil for summer flowering.
N. alata 'Lime Green'
H: 60 cm (2 ft); S: 30 cm (1 ft) ▶
Lime-green flower; sow seed in warm
greenhouse February to March. Keep
well-watered. Available in dwarf forms.

N. 'Domino Pink'
H and S: 30 cm (18 in) ▶
Bushy plants characterized by bright
magenta-pink flowers. Other colours
available in Domino Series.

Osteospermum
Genus of evergreen semi-woody
perennials. Suits a sunny aspect and
likes well-drained soil. Produces
sprawling daisy-like flowers in summer
to early autumn.
O. 'Buttermilk'
H: 60 cm (2 ft); S: 30 cm (1 ft) ▶
Large butter-yellow daisy-like flowers
with dark eyes.
O. 'Whirly Gig'
H: 60 cm (2 ft); S: 30–45 cm (12–18 in) ▶
White paddle-shaped petals.

Pelargonium 'Balcon Royale'
Trails: 30–60 cm (12–24 in) T
Perennial, trailing ivy-leaved pelargonium
with bluish-red flowers in mid-spring to
mid-autumn. Overwinter indoors and
display in dry sunny conditions.

Pelargonium 'Friesdorf'
H: 25 cm (10 in); S: 15 cm (6 in) T
Zonal evergreen perennial. Characterized
by dark green foliage and scarlet-orange
flowers with thin petals.

Nicotiana 'Domino Pink'

Osteospermum 'Whirly Gig'

Petunia

Petunia
A genus of annuals characterized by
showy flowers in a variety of colours,
either Grandiflora or Multiflora. They
need plenty of sun and well-drained soil.
P. 'Dark Blue Dwarf'
H: 20 cm (8 in) ▶
Rich blue flowers, well suited to
small pots.
P. 'Express Ruby'
H: 23–30 cm (9–12 in) ▶
Large purple flowers with dark throats.
P. surfina
H: 23–30 cm (9–12 in) ▶
Numerous named hybrids are also
available. Plant out late May to June
and dead-head to make the most of
the long flowering season.

Phlox drummondii
H: 15–30 cm (6–12 in); S: 10 cm (4 in) ▶
Annual, available in pink, mauve and red.
Plant out late May to June. Prefers moist
sunny or partially shaded conditions.

Phyllitis scolopendrium
(syn. **Asplenium scolopendrium**)
H: 30–45 cm (12–18 in); S: 45 cm (18 in) T
Fern with light green elegantly curved
fronds. Pot February to March. Water
freely March to October. Overwinter in a
greenhouse or conservatory. Prefers shade.

Pittosporum tenuifolium 'Purpureum'
H: 2 m (6 ft); S: 4 m (13 ft) T
Evergreen large shrub or small tree. Pale
green leaves gradually change to deep
bronze purple. Honey-scented flowers in
spring. Can be cut back.

Polygala myrtifolia
H and S: 1.5 m (5 ft) T
Flowering evergreen shrub with
pale green leaves and bright purple pea
flowers. Overwinter in a greenhouse
or conservatory.

Primula (Primrose)
A genus of annuals, biennials and
perennials that enjoy sunny positions and
well-drained soil. Characterized by basal
leaves and primrose-shaped flowers.
P. denticulata
H: 30–45 cm (12–18 in) ●
Perennial that comes in shades of mauve
or white with round heads on long stems
in spring and has long toothed leaves.
Works well as a single specimen.
P. polyanthus Gold Lace Group
(Gold-laced polyanthus)
H: 15–20 cm (6–8 in) ●
Spring flowering perennial with round
heads in a variety of gold edged colours. A
large number of named varieties exist,
hybridized since the mid-18th century.

P. veris (Cowslip)
H and S: 15–20 cm (6–8 in) ●
Native perennial with rounded long
leaves and small, deep yellow flowers
in long-stalked clusters in spring.
P. vulgaris
H: 15 cm (6 in); S: 25 cm (10 in) ●
Perennial with short thick leaves and pale
yellow flowers with darker centres in late
winter and spring. Looks good as a single
plant or in shallow containers in clumps.

Prunus lusitanica (Portugal laurel)
H and S: 6 m (20 ft) ●
Evergreen shrub or small tree with ovate
dark green glossy leaves and small white
hawthorn-scented flowers in June. Small
red fruits turning to dark purple in
autumn. A good subject for mop-head
standards. Tolerates shade.

Pyracantha coccinea
H and S: 4 m (12 ft) ●
Evergreen shrub, densely branched with
white flowers in large clusters in summer
followed by red or orange-red berries
in large bunches in autumn to winter.
Prune to keep a compact shape; can be
espaliered and topiarized. Tolerant of all
exposures, pollution and shade.

Rosa 'Sanders' White Rambler'

Rosa 'The Fairy'

Sempervivum tectorum

Rhododendron
H: 2–2.5 m (6–8 ft) ●

Mainly evergreen shrubs with glossy foliage. Spring to summer flowering in a range of colours. Dead-head after flowering. Prune in April to keep in shape. Good hybrids for containers are: 'Cynthia (rose-crimson), 'Cunningham's White' (white), 'Doncaster' (crimson-scarlet).

Rosa (Rose)
A genus of deciduous or semi-evergreen shrubs and scrambling climbers. Grown for flowers that are often fragrant. Plant in well-drained soil.

R. 'Sanders' White Rambler'
H: 1.2–1.5 m (4–5 ft) ●

Small scented white flowers in cascading clusters. Available as a container-grown weeping standard.

R. 'The Fairy'
H: 60 cm (2 ft); S: 120 cm (4 ft) ●

Polyantha spreading rose good for shallow containers. Produces clusters of bead-like buds that open to globular pink flowers through summer. Shade tolerant. Available as pot-grown standard and half-standard.

R. 'Nozomi'
H: 60 cm (2 ft) ●

Ground cover rose with small pearly pink to white flowers produced in abundance. Ideal for hanging over the edge of pots.

R. 'White Pet'
H: 60 cm (2 ft) ●

A 19th-century Polyantha short-growing rose producing huge trusses of pure white pompon-like blooms throughout summer. This rose will tolerate a shaded position. Available as a container-grown standard and half-standard.

Rudbeckia hirta (Cone flower)
H: 60–90 cm (2–3 ft) ●

Golden-yellow flowers with dark brown centre and long oblong leaves. Plant in a sunny position and water regularly.

Salvia farinacea 'Rhea'
H: 1 m (3 ft); S: 30 cm (1 ft) ◗

A perennial with lance-shaped mid-green leaves and violet to blue flowers, from tubular spikes. Prefers well-drained soil and a sunny position.

Sempervivum tectorum (Houseleek)
H and S: 30 cm (12 in) ●

Perennial succulent. Forms dense green mound of foliage, suitable for a dry sunny position and will survive with virtually no soil and very little water. Good cascading display that works well in architectural designs in urns.

Senecio cineraria
(syn. Cineraria maritima)
(Sea ragwort)
H and S: 30 cm (1 ft) ◗

Summer-flowering perennial. Deeply cut grey leaves and yellow flowers midsummer to autumn. 'Silver Dust' is a good non-flowering cultivar.

Tagetes erecta (African marigold)
H: 30–100 cm (1–3 ft) ◗

Annual with single yellow or orange daisy-like flowers with a long summer flowering. Plant out in May in a sunny position in well-drained soil and water regularly.

Tilia x europea (Lime)
H: up to 31 m (100 ft) ●

Deciduous tree with yellowish-white fragrant flowers and broadly ovate leaves. Easy to train in containers and can be pleached, pollarded and generally kept in shape by hard pruning in mid- to late summer. If planting a bare-rooted lime, plant between mid-autumn and spring.

Tilia platyphyllos 'Rubra'
(Red-twigged lime)
H: up to 31 m (100 ft) ●

Deciduous tree. Young shoots are bright brownish-red and make a particularly effective display in winter.

Trachelospermum jasminoides

Trachelospermum jasminoides
H and S: up to 6.5 m (21 ft) T
Slow-growing climbing shrub with narrow
oval dark, shiny green leaves and very
fragrant white flowers over a very long
period from late spring to autumn. Likes
sun and moist soil. Overwinter indoors.
Can be trained.

Verbena tenera (Italian verbena)
H: 15–45 cm (6–18 in); S: 30 cm (1 ft) ●
Summer-flowering perennial with blue
or purple fragrant flowers. Also trailing
Verbena tenuisecta f. *alba* in white. Plant
in well-drained soil in a sunny position.

Vinca minor (Lesser periwinkle)
H: 15 cm (6 in); S: 1.5 m (5 ft) ●
Evergreen trailing sub-shrub with blue
to purple small white-centred flowers.
Vinca minor 'Alba Variegata' produces
white flowers. Likes semi-shade and
moist soil.
Vinca minor 'Azurea Flore Plena'
H: 15 cm (6 in); S: 1.5 m (5 ft) ●
Evergreen trailing sub-shrub. Bright
sky-blue flowers on short flowering
shoots in spring or summer. Leaves
form a dense dark green mat. Best in
sun and moist soil.

care and maintenance

BASIC EQUIPMENT

For the gardener

Container gardening requires only a handful of tools, and most of the projects in this book can be undertaken with the bare essentials of gardening equipment.

Use a wheelbarrow for fetching and moving containers and mixing compost, and a sack truck for transporting larger containers. A stout cloth or purpose-made collecting cloth with handles saves mess when potting up and can be used to remove debris.

Indispensable hand tools include an old kitchen knife for weeding pots, a hand fork and trowel, a dibber to make holes for seeds or young plants, secateurs, sharp scissors, shears and a pruning saw.

Old garden tools are often much nicer than new ones; buy them cheaply from a second-hand dealer. Failing that, invest in some stainless steel tools, which wear well and are easy to clean.

For watering and spraying, you need a watering can and a hosepipe. Use a hand-held spray for applying foliar feed and insecticide and a measuring jug for mixing them. Gardening can be a grubby business and harsh on the hands; use special tough gardening gloves for protection.

For the woodworker

There are no complicated procedures, joints or fixings in the construction projects described in this book. If you can cut a piece of wood and screw separate pieces together, you will be able to cope.

When purchasing and cutting wood, take care to use either metric or imperial measurements, depending on which system your supplier uses. On no account mix the two methods of measurement.

Use a handsaw (crosscut) for cutting timber and plywood to size. A work bench or pair of sawhorses are useful when cutting, although you can make do with a stout table. An electric jigsaw is quick and easy, particularly for curved cuts, but a coping saw will do.

The most versatile type of hammer is the claw hammer, which has one end for driving nails in and a curved claw for removing them.

For drilling holes, use a metal brace with appropriate bits or the faster hand-held electric drill.

Most structures are secured with screws. A no. 2 screwdriver with a posidriv head is recommended for these projects. When inserting screws, use a bradawl to make a pilot hole; this marks the position and prevents the screwdriver from slipping and damaging the surface of the wood.

Other useful equipment includes a pair of 'G' cramps for holding pieces together, or keeping pieces steady when you are working on them, and a smoothing plane.

For painting

Ordinary household paintbrushes are all that is required for most of the paintwork, but for decorative details an artist's brush will give more accuracy.

Before you begin to paint, ensure that the surface is smooth and clean; a soft-bristled dusting brush works best. Use white spirit to clean the brushes.

Other general equipment that may be useful includes old rags and protective plastic sheets or paper. Exterior-grade wood filler can be used to fill cracks and indents and smoothed with sandpaper.

For metal projects

The metal constructions described in this book are comparatively simple and required only a few special items of equipment, such as a pair of tinsnips for cutting lead facings and trimmings. A hacksaw is the best instrument for cutting thicker metals.

When shaping metal, use a vice on a bench together with a lump hammer to help to bend strips. For gilding, a range of metal and transfer leaves are available.

When handling lead, wear a pair of protective gloves.

WOODWORKING

Glues and fixings

The adhesive that is recommended for use in these projects is exterior-grade PVA (polyvinyl acetate) glue. Before gluing, always make sure that surfaces are free of dust and grease. Allow the adhesive to dry overnight to achieve its full strength.

Posidriv screws are the simplest screws to fix, especially when you are using an electric screwdriver. They are usually plated to protect them from rust, and are available in a variety of sizes and types.

In procedures that involve screwing wood together, pre-drill one piece to fit the screw diameter and pilot-drill the other. If you are using an electric screwdriver in softwood, a pilot hole may not be necessary.

To protect against rust, you should use sheradized pins and galvanized nails. Pins are often used with glue to reinforce a joint. For a neat finish, punch your pin below the surface and fill in the holes with a special wood filler.

Timber

Softwood has frequently been specified for use in the projects described in this book because it is inexpensive and relatively easy to work. Before applying any other finish, treat the softwood with a clear exterior-grade wood preservative.

Timber is available for purchase in either sawn (rough) or planed (smooth) finishes. It is important to inform your timber merchant which type you want because the dimensions vary.

The final width and depth of a piece of planed timber will be about 3 to 5 mm ($^1/8$ to $^3/16$ in) less than the size quoted by a supplier. This is because a 50 x 25 mm (2 x 1 in) piece of sawn timber is the size you actually get, whereas in the case of planed timber the dimensions quoted reflect the size of the timber before it has been planed.

On the whole, a sawn finish is preferable if you are using a decorative stain on your timber, because the stain has more of a key to the timber. A planed finish is more effective for a wood that is destined to be painted – such a finish is essential if you are intending to apply a gloss paint.

Plywood

Plywood is available in thicknesses ranging from 3 mm ($^1/8$ in) to 30 mm ($1^3/16$ in). The cheapest exterior-grade plywood is shuttering ply.

The alternatives include waterproof Far Eastern ply, which has a reddish tint (this can distort the colour of a stain finish), and marine ply, which is an expensive high-quality structural wood and is only worth using with hardwood.

Hardwood

Oak and teak are the best hardwood timbers for using outside, but they are expensive and hard to work. It is advisable to use a stained finish with oak and teak because it is difficult to make paint stay on these woods in the long term.

PAINTS AND STAINS

Paints

A wide range of paint types is available for exterior use on wood, including oil-based gloss, microporous exterior paint and ordinary exterior emulsion, which is long-lasting. Oil undercoat used on its own is good for a very flat finish.

Ordinary water-based paint is effective on terracotta, as is oil-bound or water-bound distemper, which can be used watered down to achieve a 'distressed' appearance. Concrete also takes emulsion paint or special exterior-grade masonry paint. For metal, use a gloss paint or a proprietary metal paint.

Stains

Some stains contain preservatives, others are only water-repellent. Stains tend to look better in muted colours and are affected by the colour of the wood to which you are applying them; they work most effectively on a sawn timber finish.

Preservatives

Unpreserved wood should be treated with anti-rot, anti-woodworm and fungicide; clear wood preservatives are available for this purpose. These are toxic to plants so they must be applied well in advance of planting.

There are some preservatives made specifically for horticultural work, but many of them are tinted, which can affect the colour of a stain applied on top.

CHOOSING A CONTAINER

When deciding what sort of containers would be most appropriate for your garden, you can either start by choosing the plants and find containers suited to the nature and habit of the plants, or start with the containers and devise planning schemes to suit them. The latter approach may have advantages in that the containers will be there all year round and will have to fit in with the character and scale of the setting.

Consider where in the garden you need plant interest and what sort of container would look good in that position. To be appreciated from a distance, the container needs to be bold and simple in outline. The height of the planting must also be decided in relation to the rest of the garden; generally, the taller the planting the larger the container needed.

Elaborate detail is best in a foreground position where it can be seen clearly, and the same applies to planting – complex schemes using delicate plants are best seen close to, where their detail can be fully appreciated.

The colour of your material should be chosen to harmonize with the house and the rest of the garden as well as with the intended planting scheme. As a general

rule, materials that weather and patinate are more appealing; hand-thrown terracotta patinates the quickest. Lead, stone and cast stone also patinate with age, and the process can be speeded up by applying vinegar in the case of lead, and yoghurt, milk or liquid manure in the case of stone and cast stone. One way to age a pot quickly is to place it under the drip of trees.

Cast iron and wood both need to be painted or stained to preserve them. Use a faded blue-grey-green, referred to as 'Versailles blue', a colour often seen on the shutters of old houses in Italy and France.

LOOKING AFTER CONTAINERS

Containers need to be scrupulously cleaned and scrubbed before planting; scrub them well on the inside with clean water but try to preserve the patina on the outside. Some containers are best used with plastic liners, especially if you change your schemes with the seasons. Plastic liners are particularly useful for large Versailles cases and urns. Check that your terracotta is frost-proof if you are going to leave it outside all year round. In winter even hardy plants in pots will need their roots protecting against severe frost – wrap the pot with hessian (as shown below),

straw or bubble wrap. Where plants are in liners, pack straw between the plastic pot and container for protection. In early autumn or spring, examine the condition of your containers and repaint them if necessary.

All containers need good drainage. Ensure that there are enough holes to let out excess moisture and put in a thin layer of pot shards or gravel in the base of pots.

PLANTING MEDIUM

Different plants need different composts. For semi-permanent plantings use an aerated nutritious compost, and for short-term schemes a soil-less multi-purpose compost. Some plants have specific needs. For instance, special composts are available for bulbs, and very gritty free-draining soil-based composts are recommended for some alpine and rock plants. John Innes composts are numbered 1, 2 and 3 according to their nutritional content. Note whether your plant needs a fast or slow growing medium.

Peat-based mixtures are appropriate for containers because they are light, but they also have a tendency to dry out, so are unsuitable for plants that are difficult to water. Loam-based mixtures offer a more stable alternative but carry more weight. Also available are bark, coir and wood-fibre composts that work well in containers.

POTTING PLANTS

The size of the pot should complement the size of the planting and needs to be large enough to contain the rootball and sustain growth. Some plants dislike being repotted repeatedly and do not mind being root-bound, whereas others need to be regularly potted on as they grow. Most seasonal plantings, if properly fed and

watered, can stand being in a confined pot. For a shrub or tree, start off with a large container that will support its growth for a number of years before the inevitable repotting. Some Versailles cases are specifically designed for ease of repotting; the sides let down for easy removal of the root ball. Such a design might be suitable for large plants such as orange and lemon trees, camellias and greenhouse exotics.

When potting up a multiple seasonal planting, you may need to cram in the depotted root balls to create the desired effect. This would not be appropriate for permanent plantings but in this case, as long as the roots have space to develop downwards, the plants will survive.

For permanent plantings, take extra care with root-ball placement. Single specimens should be placed centrally in the pot and firmed down. Make sure the soil surface is at least 25 mm (1 in) below the top edge of the pot so that there is space for a water reservoir. In the case of standards, choose a specimen with an upright and secure stem (stake if required) because it is hard to correct this later.

Climbing plants can have supports fixed in the soil or to the container – there are a wide range of stakes, metal shapes, and trellis obelisks available which you can construct yourself or buy ready-made.

WATERING

In summer, the key to successful container gardening is regular watering. Small pots, particularly those made of terracotta, dry out very quickly, and during spells of hot weather they will need watering twice a day – in the early morning and in the evening, to avoid sunburn to wet leaves. Water larger pots only once a day. Always soak the plant thoroughly by filling the reservoir at the top up to the brim. If

you are using a hose, use one with a rose end so that the water pressure does not wash away any compost.

Reduce watering as the growing season ends. In winter most plants need only to be kept from drying out, so check them every few days to make sure they are still moist. Some plants that are dormant in winter prefer the soil to be almost dry – check individual plants for special needs. A useful way to conserve moisture is to place a layer of mulch over the soil.

FEEDING

There are various methods for feeding pot-grown plants. Slow-release granules are good for long-term plantings – sprinkle them onto the surface of the soil and rake them into the compost. Other chemical feeds can be mixed into the compost when planting. Liquid feeds are diluted in water and used as part of the watering regime. Foliar feeds are sprayed on for instant effect, and organic material can be used as a top dressing. Use home-made compost, well-rotted manure or blood and bone, applied during the growing season.

When planting, always follow the specific feed requirements because some plants like a relatively impoverished soil and do not respond well to overfeeding.

PESTS AND DISEASES

Plants that are stressed as a consequence of poor watering and feeding are more vulnerable to attack – so the surest way to prevent the invasion of pests and diseases is to take the best possible care of your plants and containers. Cleanliness of pots and tools helps to keep bacterial diseases at bay, as does keeping a regular eye on their health.

Plants are vulnerable to three groups of diseases: bacterial, fungal and viral. Viral diseases are untreatable – destruction of the plant is the only remedy.

Above is a typical example of bacterial leaf spot (left) and powdery mildew (right). Benomyl is the most useful spray for bacterial leaf spot, black spot, fungal leaf spot and powdery mildew; spray only on calm days after sunset so as not to harm beneficial insects.

The most common pests to attack container plants are aphids (greenfly and blackfly); these can be sprayed with pirimicarb. Whitefly can be treated with permethrin, and scale insects with a mixture of liquid paraffin and nicotine.

Always take care to store garden sprays and chemicals well out of the reach of children and pets – and wear gloves and a mask as directed.

useful addresses

PAINTS AND STAINS

Farrow and Ball
Uddens Estate, Wimborne
Dorset BH21 7NI
01202 876141
www.farrow-ball.com

John Oliver Ltd
33 Pembridge Road
London W11 3HG
020 7221 6466

Sadolin
Meadow Lane, St Ives
Cambridgeshire PE27 4UY
01480 496868
www.sadolin.co.uk

NURSERIES

Blooms of Bressingham
Dorney Court
Dorney, Windsor
Berkshire SL4 6QP
01628 669999
*And at nine other locations in
southern and central England.*

Capital Gardens
Alexandra Palace Garden Centre
Alexandra Palace Way
London N22 7BB
020 8444 2555
www.capitalgardens.co.uk

The Chelsea Gardener
125 Sydney Street
London SW3 6NR
020 7352 5656

Craven's Nursery
1 Foulds Terrace, Bingley
West Yorkshire BD10 4LZ
01274 561412

Deacons Nursery
Moor View, Godshill
Isle of Wight PO38 3HW
01983 840750

Finchley Nurseries
Burton Hole Lane
London NW7 1AS
020 8959 2124

Garson Farm Garden Centre
Winterdown Road, Esher
Surrey KT10 8LS
01372 460181

Highfield Nurseries
Whitminster
Gloucester
Gloucestershire GL2 7PL
01452 740266

Longacres Nursery
London Road, Bagshot
Surrey GU19 5JB
01276 476778

Potterton & Martin
Moortown Road, Nettleton
Market Rasen
Lincolnshire LN7 6HX
01472 851714

The Romantic Garden Nursery
Swannington
Norwich
Norfolk NR9 5NW
01603 261488
www.romantic-garden-nursery.co.uk

Scotts Nurseries
Merriott
Somerset TA16 5PL
01460 72306

Syon Park Garden Centre
Syon Park
Brentford
Middlesex TW8 8JG
020 8568 7776

The Van Hage Garden Co.
Bragbury End
Stevenage
Hertfordshire SG2 8TJ
01438 811777

Wyevale Garden Centres
Waddon Way
Purley Way
Croydon CR0 4HY
020 8688 5117

TERRACOTTA AND STONEWARE

Barbary Pots
45 Fernshaw Road
London SW10 0TN
020 7352 1053

Chilstone
Victoria Park
Fordcombe
Kent TN3 0RD
01892 740866

Christie's
8 King Street
London SW1Y 6QT
020 7839 9060

Crafts Council Directory
44a Pentonville Road
London N1 9BY
020 7278 7700

Cranborne Stone
West Orchard
Shaftesbury
Dorset SP7 0LF
01258 472685

Pots and Pithoi
The Barns, East Street
Turners Hill
West Sussex RH10 4QQ
01342 714793

Whichford Pottery
Whichford
Shipston-on-Stour
Warwickshire CV36 5PG
01608 684416

PLANTERS AND GARDEN STRUCTURES

Baileys Home & Garden
The Engine Shed
Ashburton Industrial Estate
Ross-on-Wye
Herefordshire HR9 7BW
01989 563015

Bulbeck Foundry
Reach Road, Burwell
Cambridgeshire CB5 0AH
01638 743153

Exmoor Baskets & Hurdles
The SCC Highways Depot
Station Road, Dulverton
Somerset TA22 9AD
01398 323391

George Carter
Silverstone Farm
North Elmham
Norfolk NR20 5EX
01362 668130

Interior Landscaping Products
The Sussex Barn
New Lodge Farm
Hooe, Battle
East Sussex TN33 9HJ
01424 844444
www.interiorlandscaping.co.uk

Rayment Wirework
Hoo Farm, Monkton Road
Ramsgate
Kent CT12 4EA
01843 821628

Stuart Garden Architecture
Burrow Hill Farm
Wiveliscombe
Somerset TA4 2RN
01984 667458

Terrace and Garden
Maces Farm
Rickling Green
Saffron Walden
Essex CB11 3YG
01799 543289

TIMBER AND BUILDING SUPPLIES

B & Q
Portswood House
Chandlers Ford
Eastleigh
Hampshire SO53 3RY
023 8025 6256
www.diy.com
Over 320 stores nationwide.

Homebase
0870 900 8098
www.homebase.co.uk
Over 300 stores nationwide.

E. K. Wilson & Sons
87 Old Brompton Road
London SW7 3LD
020 7589 0046

The York Handmade Brick Company
Winchester House
Forest Lane, Alne
North Yorkshire YO61 1TU
01347 838881
www.yorkhandmade.co.uk

index

credits

The projects in this book were designed by George Carter, except for Vertical Planting (pages 24–27) and A Wirework Hanging Basket (pages 58–61), both of which were designed by Jane Seabrook at The Chelsea Gardener. Much of the planting was lent by John Powles at the Romantic Garden Nursery, Swannington, Norfolk. All the photographs were taken by Marianne Majerus, except for page 45 bottom right, which was taken by Francesca Yorke at an Islington garden designed by Diana Yakeley, Yakeley Associates Design, Interior and Garden Design, 13 College Cross, London N1 1YY (020 7609 9846) dy@yakeley.com.

acknowledgments

The author would like to thank the many people involved in making this book,
particularly Marianne Majerus for her wonderful photographs, John Powles and
The Romantic Garden Nursery for the loan of plants, and Jane Seabrook and
The Chelsea Gardener for planting and use of the nursery.

The following people kindly lent their own beautiful gardens as backdrops for photography:
Mrs David Cargill, Ethne Clarke, Mr and Mrs Robert Clarke, Viscount and Viscountess De L'Isle,
Major Charles Fenwick, Mrs Clive Hardcastle, Mr and Mrs Derek Howard, Anne Ryland,
Jacqui Small, The Lady Tollemache and Mr and Mrs Richard Winch.

Thanks also go to Jill Duchess of Hamilton for lending urns, to Jill Hamer for typing
the text, and to Peter Goodwins and Jack Bell for construction and bricklaying.

The first edition of this book was edited by Toria Leitch and designed by Ingunn Jensen.